RAND NATIONAL DEFENSE RESEARCH INSTITUTE

T0308517

Spillover from the Conflict in Syria

An Assessment of the Factors that Aid and Impede the Spread of Violence

William Young, David Stebbins, Bryan A. Frederick,
Omar Al-Shahery

Prepared for the Office of the Secretary of Defense

For more information on this publication, visit www.rand.org/t/rr609

Library of Congress Cataloging-in-Publication Data is available for this publication.

Published by the RAND Corporation, Santa Monica, Calif.
© Copyright 2014 RAND Corporation
RAND® is a registered trademark.

Cover image: Iraqi Shiite tribal fighters in Baghdad, Iraq (AP photo/Karim Kadim).

Support RAND
Make a tax-deductible charitable contribution at
www.rand.org/giving/contribute

www.rand.org

Preface

All roads lead to Damascus and then back out again but in different directions. The financial and military aid flowing into Syria from patrons and neighbors is intended to determine the outcome of the conflict between a loose confederation of rebel factions and the regime in Damascus. Instead, this outside support has the potential to perpetuate the existing civil war and to ignite larger regional hostilities between Sunni and Shia areas that could reshape the political geography of the Middle East. This study examines the main factors that are likely to contribute to or impede the spread of violence from civil war and insurgency and then examines how they apply to Turkey, Lebanon, Iraq, and Jordan.

This research was conducted within the International Security and Defense Policy Center of the RAND National Defense Research Institute, a federally funded research and development center sponsored by the Office of the Secretary of Defense, the Joint Staff, the Unified Combatant Commands, the Navy, the Marine Corps, the defense agencies, and the defense Intelligence Community.

For more information on the International Security and Defense Policy Center, see http://www.rand.org/nsrd/ndri/centers/isdp.html or contact the director (contact information is provided on the web page).

Contents

Summary

For the purpose of this study, spillover refers to the spread of violent conflict and its ramifications from civil war in Syria between the Alawite regime of Bashar Al-Assad in Damascus and its disjointed, albeit committed, rebel opposition. The study identifies the main factors that are likely to contribute to or impede the spread of violence from civil war and insurgency and then examines how they apply to Turkey, Lebanon, Iraq, and Jordan.

The literature on armed conflict shows that the following factors contribute directly to the spread of violence from civil war and insurgency:

- External military support
- Large numbers of refugees
- Fragility of neighboring states.

Additional factors are:

- Ethnic ties
- Access to open media
- Perceived uncertainty and government overreaction by neighbors
- Timing and effectiveness of intervention
- Government and insurgent capabilities.

Preventing the spillover of violence requires:

- Early intervention to either negotiate or impose a settlement.

- Working with neighboring states and allies to stem the flow of foreign fighters and external aid.
- Working with neighboring states and allies to prevent the influx of refugees into those states and to provide safe zones for their return.
- Military and financial assistance to the neighboring states (not to the warring parties) to secure borders and inoculate neighboring states from the instability that accompanies the spread of radical ideologies, economic hardship, and war.

All of the factors leading to the spread of violent conflict from civil war and insurgency currently are present in varying degrees in the Levant. There is a high probability that, if left unchecked, the sectarian fighting in Syria will spill over into Turkey and Jordan. Violence has already spilled into Lebanon and Iraq.

To impede the spillover of violence now occurring in Lebanon and Iraq and to reverse the likelihood of it spreading into Turkey and Jordan, it will be necessary to address the underlying causes of the spillover in the region by:

- Negotiating with and persuading the Arab Gulf states, Iran, and Russia to curtail their military assistance to the rebels and the regime.
- Negotiating or imposing a ceasefire to permit the time and space needed to set up safe zones and protected, safe-passage corridors so refugees can return and humanitarian aid can be provided. These measures are likely to require the presence of some type of international stabilization force.

Acknowledgments

We wish to thank our reviewers, Andrew Liepman and Michael McHenry, for their thoughtful and thorough reading of the manuscript. Their recommendations and insights contributed significantly to the study. We also want to thank Andria Tyner for her extensive administrative assistance.

Abbreviations

AQI	al-Qaida in Iraq
FSA	Free Syrian Army
ISIS	Islamic State of Iraq and Syria
KRG	Kurdish Regional Government
LAF	Lebanese Armed Forces
PKK	Kurdistan Worker's Party
PYD	Kurdish Democratic Union Party
UNHCR	United Nations High Commissioner for Refugees

Prologue

Since the completion of this study in early fall 2013, the political and humanitarian fallout from the Syrian conflict has begun to dramatically change the landscape of the Middle East: The violence from fighting in Syria has spread wider and more deeply into the region, threatening each of the surrounding countries, and it has grown into a larger sectarian battle between Sunnis and Shia that is radicalizing the youth and otherwise secular populations in the region. These trends were forecast in 2013 in the following pages, which we have updated to reflect the gradual yet inevitable rise of the Islamic State of Iraq and Syria (ISIS) and the rapid spread of their fighters' control of the Sunni regions of eastern Syria and western Iraq.

Time, as the original study pointed out, is a key factor when considering the potential spread of violence from an insurgency into surrounding areas. It is rare that situations like these remain static, especially when there is so much instability in the region and so much religious commitment on both sides of the struggle. In short, what can be done with a given policy today cannot be done tomorrow or certainly will be more difficult to do.

The ability of ISIS to sweep through northern Iraq has been a direct outgrowth of the time and space it had since the start of the Syrian conflict to establish itself geographically, politically, and militarily in eastern Syria. By focusing on Bashar Al-Assad and his regime in Damascus, the United States and its allies lost an opportunity to crush this new jihadist phenomenon in its infancy. It will now be much harder to do and will require, as the original study suggested, engaging with Tehran, Moscow, and the regime in Damascus. After all, Assad has never posed a threat to the West or the Arab Gulf States, whereas ISIS and other al-Qaida affiliates have threatened the region's stability and U.S. allies in the region from the beginning of the Syrian conflict. This is where the focus should be, and it is the direction taken for the analysis in the following pages.

Finding a solution to the current spillover of fighting from Syria into Iraq and preventing the violence from spreading further into Jordan, Lebanon, Turkey, and the Kurdish regions will require recognizing the following geopolitical realities on the ground:

- Syria and Iraq are no longer the geographic entities we have known; both are now de facto partitioned states.
- The conflict that began in opposition to Assad in Damascus has become a wider religious struggle between Sunni and Shia in the region.
- The potential for the conflict to spread further into surrounding states and the Arab Gulf is high.
- The continued radicalization of youth in the region is the greatest threat to the region's future stability.
- The solution will require negotiating with the regimes in Damascus, Iran, and Russia to arrange an armistice.
- A stop to the fighting will require an end to external military aid to groups inside Syria.
- Refugees need to return to safe areas within Syria that are protected, at least in the short term, by an international stabilization force.
- An end to the fighting in Syria will enable the international community to focus on dismantling ISIS, which has now declared itself "The Islamic State."
- It seems unlikely Iraq and Syria will return to how they were before; the people within those countries are no longer likely to accept the authority of central governments in Damascus and Baghdad.
- A divided-state solution, along the lines of the Dayton Accords in Bosnia, should be considered both for Syria and Iraq as a way to help reshape the narrative for the region.

CHAPTER ONE

Introduction

All roads lead to Damascus and then back out again but in different directions. The financial and military aid flowing into Syria from patrons and neighbors such as Iran, Russia, Libya, Saudi Arabia, Qatar, and other Arab Gulf states is intended to determine the outcome of the conflict between a loose confederation of rebel factions and the Bashar Al-Assad regime.[1] Instead, this outside support has the potential to perpetuate the existing civil war within the country and ignite larger regional hostilities between Sunni and Shia areas that could reshape the political geography of the Middle East. In many ways, this is the perfect jihad,[2] pitting Sunni against Shia in a continuation of the long struggle for dominance in the Islamic world. We already are beginning to see the historical hatreds between extremists on both sides of the conflict spill over, spreading fear and influencing political sentiment and opportunism north and east into Turkey and Iraq, west into Lebanon, Israel, and Palestine, and south into Jordan and the Arab Gulf.[3]

---

[1] William Young, *The Winners and Losers From The Syria Conflict,* cnn.com, January 21, 2013; and Jeffrey Martini, Erin York, William Young, *Syria as an Arena of Strategic Competition,* Santa Monica, Calif.: RAND Corporation, RR-213-OSD, 2013.

[2] This concept is adapted from Nibras Kazimi, *Syria Through Jihadist Eyes: A Perfect Enemy,* Stanford: Hoover Institution Press, 2010; and Fouad Ajami, *The Syrian Rebellion,* Stanford: Hoover Institution Press, 2012.

[3] "Israel: al-Qaeda Plot Against U.S. Embassy Alleged," *Washington Post,* January 23, 2014. See also "Iraq: Strikes Spread Beyond Anbar," *New York Times,* February 12, 2014, p. 6; and Hwaida Saad and Ben Hubbard's discussion of violence spreading in Lebanon in "Lebanon Forms a Cabinet After 11 Months of Deadlock," *New York Times,* February 16, 2014, p. 8; and "4 Killed in Twin Suicide Blasts in Beirut," *Washington Post,* February 2014, p. 10.

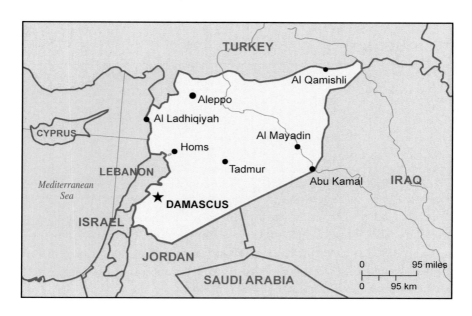

The region's histories, memories, and ethnicities are never far from the surface of the terrain, and to understand the potential for violent spillover from these trends, we have examined the region as a dynamic whole, taking into consideration the human geography, political culture, and histories of the participants as they vie for power and a larger share of land and resources. Each of the factors cited in this report must be viewed in this context and in combination as part of a cumulative whole.[4]

In medical research, "spillover" is the moment when a pathogen passes from one species into another. It is a focused event; unlike "emergence," in which the incidence of infection increases following introduction into a new host. Spillover leads to emergence when a virus or other disease infects members of a new host, thrives, and spreads.[5]

---

[4] For additional information, see Kristian Skrede Gleditsch, *All International Politics is Local,* Ann Arbor: The University of Michigan Press, 2002; David Lake and Donald S. Rothchild, *The International Spread of Ethnic Conflict: Fear, Diffusion, and Escalation,* Princeton: Princeton University Press, 1998; Richard Herrmann and Jong Kun Choi, "From Prediction to Learning: Opening Experts' Minds to Unfolding History," *International Security,* Spring 2007, p. 132.

[5] This definition is drawn from David Quammen, *Spillover: Animal Infections and the Next Pandemic,* New York: W.W. Norton & Company, 2012, p. 43. See also Hank Houweling and

The spread of violent conflict is similar in many ways to the spread of an infectious disease, either within given cultures and populations or between them. Like a virus, extremist ideologies, ethnic sentiment, and religious anger know no boundaries. Refugee flows bring ideologies and transmit anger that radicalizes youth and neighboring populations who share lineage and language. Geography provides access and facilitates the further spread of these ideas along with the movement of people and weapons.[6] The contagion can spread easily into the body of adjoining societies where conditions already may be fragile.

For the purpose of this report, *spillover* refers to the spread of violent conflict and its ramifications from civil war in Syria between the Alawite regime of Bashar Al-Assad in Damascus and its disjointed, albeit committed, rebel opposition. We identify the main factors that are likely to contribute to or impede the spread of violence from civil war and insurgency and then examine how they apply to Turkey, Lebanon, Iraq, and Jordan.

Jan Siccama, "The Epidemiology of War, 1816–1980," *Journal of Conflict Resolution*, Vol. 29, 1985, pp. 641–662; and Kelly Keclera, "Transmission, Barriers, and Constraints: A Dynamic Model of the Spread of War," *Journal of Conflict Resolution*, Vol. 42, 1998, pp. 367–387.

[6] For further information on the spillover of political conflict see Daniel Byman and Kenneth Pollack, *Things Fall Apart: Containing the Spillover from an Iraqi Civil War*, Washington, D.C.: Brookings Institution Press, 2007; and Byman, Daniel, Peter Chalk, Bruce Hoffman, William Rosenau, and David Brannan, *Trends in Outside Support for Insurgent Movements*, Santa Monica, Calif.: RAND Corporation, MR-1405-OTI, 2001.

CHAPTER TWO

Review of the Literature Concerning Conflict Spillover

A review of academic literature on armed conflict and its spread into neighboring countries shows that the following factors are most likely to contribute to the spillover of violence.

External Support/Military. One of the most significant contributors to conflict spillover is external support or international intervention. Not only does the act of external support (either to nation state or opposition) increase the probability of a conflict spreading, but it may also increase the duration of the conflict.[1] Once a third party enters into the conflict on either side, the opposing side will regard it as an additional enemy that seeks to disrupt the balance of battle. Conflict spillover can be observed historically in the cases of Uganda, Bosnia, Nicaragua, Nagorno-Karabakh, and the Sudan, as well as more recently in Afghanistan, Libya, and Lebanon.[2]

Scholarly debates persist regarding whether international (or any type of third-party) intervention increases or decreases the actual duration of the conflict in question.[3] Research has centered on the timing of interventions and whether the "ripeness" of the conflict has reached a

---

[1] Tony Addison and S. Mansoob Murshed, *Transnational Terrorism as a Spillover of Domestic Disputes in Other Countries,* World Institute for Development Economics, December 2002. See, also, Patrick M. Regan, "Third-Party Interventions and the Duration of Intrastate Conflicts," *Journal of Conflict Resolution,* Vol. 46, 2002.

[2] Kyle Beardsley, "Peacekeeping and the Contagion of Armed Conflict," *The Journal of Politics,* Vol. 73, No. 4, October 2011, pp. 1051–1064.

[3] Regan, 2002.

"mutually hurting stalemate."[4] These particular debates, however interesting, are beyond the scope of this brief study. More important is that scholars believe multilateral intervention, as opposed to unilateral action, may prove more fruitful for the peaceful resolution of the conflict in the long run,[5] and that decisive unilateral action may be more beneficial in preventing the spillover of violence early on.[6]

Refugee/Population Movements. A second significant factor that contributes to the conflict spillover is the exodus of civilians from the country in turmoil. Such movements directly and detrimentally affect the receiving nation. Some scholars posit that refugee movements may not just be the effect of an ongoing civil war but also may be the cause in many cases.[7]

While the exact mechanism by which refugee movements become civil wars or insurgencies remains under investigation, the correlation between the two is clear. The historical record is replete with examples: Liberia and Sierra Leone, Guinea and Cote d'Ivoire, the Balkans, Rwanda, and the Democratic Republic of the Congo.[8]

Refugee encampments can be detrimental economically to first-destination nation states.[9] Not only do these types of population move-

---

[4]   Kristian Skrede Gleditsch, "Fighting at Home, Fighting Abroad: How Civil Wars Lead to International Disputes," *Journal of Conflict Resolution,* April 1, 2008. See Richard N. Haass, "Ripeness of Conflict: A Fruitful Notion?" *Journal of Peace Research,* Vol. 31, No. 1, February 1994, pp. 109–116; Stephen J. Stedman, *Peacemaking in Civil War: International Mediation in Zimbabwe,* 1974–1980, Lynne Rienner Publishers, 1991; I. William Zartman, *Ripe for Resolution: Conflict and Intervention in Africa,* Oxford University Press, 1989; Marieke Kleiboer. "Ripeness of Conflict: A Fruitful Notion?" (review), *Journal of Peace Research,* Vol. 31, No. 1, February 1994, pp. 109–116.

[5]   Byman and Pollack, 2007, p. xviii.

[6]   Regan, 2002; Richard Betts, "The Delusion of Impartial Intervention," *Foreign Affairs,* November/December 1994; Paul Collier et al., "On the Duration of Civil War," *Journal of Peace Research,* Vol. 41, No. 3, May, 2004, pp. 253–273.

[7]   Idean Salehyan and Kristian Skrede Gleditsch, "Refugees and the Spread of Civil War," *International Organization,* Vol. 60, No. 2, April 2006, pp. 335–366

[8]   Salehyan and Gleditsch 2006, p. 338.

[9]   James C. Murdoch and Todd Sandler, " Economic Growth, Civil Wars, and Spatial Spillovers," *Journal of Conflict Resolution,* 2002, pp. 91–110.

ments cause neighboring states to divert resources away from state capacity building and core infrastructure planning, opposition forces may find solace within such encampments that also serve as fertile recruiting grounds for insurgencies and for establishing a viable weapons supply route.[10] Both of these phenomena can be observed currently in the Levant. Jordan has been hit particularly hard with infrastructure issues and a dwindling water supply,[11] while Sunni refugee populations may further tip the sectarian balance in Lebanon and contribute toward a re-emergence of civil war. Refugee populations are given preferential treatment, compared to minority Lebanese populations. This reinforces a negative view of the influx.[12]

Fragility of Neighboring States. The relative stability of governing institutions in states bordering conflict areas is a third primary factor leading to the spread of violence. Authors point out that the perception of spreading conflict can lead to greater oppression at home, causing a form of preemptive repression. Unstable regimes in Africa situated next to countries in conflict, for example, are likely to experience conflict themselves.[13] Moreover, scholars have argued that the type of border (such as one easily crossed) may further promote regional instability by further weakening already fragile states.[14]

---

[10] Nathan Danneman and Emily Hencken Ritter, "Contagious Rebellion and Preemptive Repression," *Journal of Conflict Resolution*, January 20, 2013, p. 3.

[11] Joby Warrick, "Influx of Syrian Refugees Stretches Jordan's Water Resources Even More Thinly," *Washington Post*, June 16, 2013.

[12] Faysal Itani, "Beyond Spillover: Syria's Role in Lebanon's Drift Toward Political Violence," Atlantic Counsel Issue Brief , July 2013.

[13] Maarten Bosker and Joppe de Reey, *Localizing Conflict Spillovers: Introducing Regional Heterogeneity in Conflict Studies,* University of Groningen, 2009.

[14] See Boaz Atzili, "When Good Fences Make Bad Neighbors: Fixed Borders, State Weakness, and International Conflict," *International Security*, Vol. 31, No. 3, Winter 2006/07, pp. 139–173; and Friedrich Kratochwil, "Of Systems, Boundaries, and Territoriality: An Inquiry into the Formation of the State System," *Politics*, Vol. 39, No. 1, October 1986, pp. 27–52.

The type of government and its respective state capacity may also contribute to spillover.[15] Further quantitative data are needed to assist in differentiating between "direct" and" indirect" diffusion and the impact it may have on neighboring countries due to the type of the government.[16] One author takes care to note that since governments remain in a constant state of evolution,[17] many of the previously established government mechanisms, once destroyed, are nearly impossible to replace in any reasonable timeframe, leading to the outbreak of new conflict and possible spillover.[18] In short, states that are more capable are able to manage refugee populations and other tasks, whereas states with poor capacity are unable to do so and, therefore, are much more affected by the negative aspects of such phenomena.

Additional Factors from the Literature that Contribute to Conflict Spillover

External support, refugee populations, and the fragility of neighboring states were the most prominent factors cited in the literature; however, scholars have also cited additional variables as contributors to conflict spillover.

Ethnic Linkages. Shared ethnicity is a key variable when assessing the prospects for conflict spilling across borders within a given region. The literature has correlated ethnic linkages not only to the spread of conflict by way of cross-cultural and outside support but also in raising collective awareness among opposition groups. For instance,

---

[15] See Alex Braithwaite, "Resisting Infection: How State Capacity Conditions Conflict Contagion," *Journal of Peace Research,* Vol. 47, No. 3, 2010, pp. 311–319; Jessica Maves, "Autocratic Institutions and Civil Conflict Contagion," *The Journal of Politics,* Vol. 75, No. 2, April 2013, pp. 478–490.

[16] Stephen M. Saideman, "When Conflict Spreads: Arab Spring and the Limits of Contagion," *International Interactions,* Vol. 37, No. 5, 2012.

[17] This is the case even when autocracies are removed violently by opposition forces. See Alexander S. Gard-Murray and Yaneer Bar-Yam, "Complexity and the Limits of Revolution: What Will Happen to the Arab Spring?" *New England Complex Systems Institute,* December 11, 2012.

[18] Gard-Murray and Bar-Yam, 2012.

violence against certain groups in neighboring states may raise awareness at home or raise intrastate expectations of their government in terms of fair treatment or representation.[19] This point has been illustrated statistically and empirically by examining the Tuareg rebels in Mali and Niger, and the Afar rebel groups in both Ethiopia and Djibouti.[20] Other cases in the literature include the Albanian population in Kosovo,[21] the Kurds in Iraq,[22] and dispersed Palestinian populations, among others.

Internal ethnic divisions within neighboring states, especially over long periods of time, may significantly contribute to spillover.[23] Ethnic divisions have been quantitatively tested and shown to be important in explaining both the onset of conflict and the creation of insurgencies.[24] Regime political figures may sometimes act to deter certain ethnic communities from siding with opposition forces.[25]

Access to Open Media. In the literature, a clear distinction has been made between direct and indirect transmission concerning possible mechanisms for the spread of conflict.[26] Conflict can spread directly via refugees, whereas social media and access to other open media services can have a more indirect impact. Some have argued that technology (or new media) alone may not be enough to tip the balance

---

[19] Halvard Buhaug and Kristian Skrede Gleditsch, "Contagion or Confusion? Why Conflicts Cluster in Space," *International Studies Quarterly,* 2008, pp. 215–233. Also see Lake and Rothchild, 1998, p. 424.

[20] Erika Forsberg, "Polarization and Ethnic Conflict in a Widened Strategic Setting," *Journal of Peace Research,* Vol. 45, No. 2, 2008, pp. 283–300.

[21] Buhaug and Gleditsch, 2008

[22] W. Andrew Terrill, "Regional Spillover Effects of the Iraq War," *Strategic Studies Institute,* December 2008.

[23] Dan Braha, "Global Civil Unrest: Contagion, Self-Organization, and Prediction," *PLoS ONE,* Vol. 7, No. 10, October 2012.

[24] See Nicholas Sambanis, "What Is Civil War? Conceptual and Empirical Complexities of an Operational Definition," *Journal of Conflict Resolution,* Vol. 48, 2004; and: J. D Fearon and D.D. Laitin, "Ethnicity, Insurgency, and Civil War," *American Political Science Review,* 2003, pp. 75–90.

[25] See Martini, York, and Young, 2013; and Young, 2013.

[26] Saideman, 2012.

leading to civil revolt,[27] while others have pointed to its direct effect and ability to contribute to the learning cycle of other populations.[28] While it is not the purpose of this analysis to focus on the viability of uprisings triggered by social media, [29] exposure to such open technologies may have a multiplier effect and add to the conditions necessary for conflict spillover.[30]

Perceived Uncertainty. Not knowing and perhaps fearing the outcome of a neighboring conflict often leads state actors to behave either more offensively or more defensively. Defensive action may come in the form of further internal repression to prevent a possible spillover,[31] while offensive action may come in the form of direct intervention to either facilitate negotiation or to quickly bring about a decisive end to the neighboring conflict. Perceptions of vulnerability have long led state actors to behave in a manner they perceive as beneficial but that, in fact, exacerbates tensions within their own societies.[32] The offensive or defensive actions of an already fragile state may only serve to further weaken the actor to the point where spillover becomes inevitable.[33]

---

[27] Armando Salvatore, "Before (and After) the 'Arab Spring': From Connectedness to Mobilization in the Public Sphere," *Oriente Moderno,* Vol. 91, No. 1, 2011, pp. 5–12.

[28] See Habibul Haque Khondker, "Role of the New Media in the Arab Spring," Zayed University, Abu Dhabi, United Arab Emirates. November 18, 2011.

[29] See Sheri Berman, "The Promise of the Arab Spring In Political Development, No Gain Without Pain," *Foreign Affairs,* January/February 2013; and Seth Jones, "The Mirage of the Arab Spring," *Foreign Affairs,* Vol. 92, No. 1, January 2013, pp. 55–63.

[30] It should be understood that the intended or unintended consequence (or positive or negative effect) is open to interpretation by the receiving group. See Saideman, 2012; Manus I. Midlarsky, "Analyzing Diffusion and Contagion Effects: The Urban Disorders of the 1960s," *American Political Science Review,* Vol. 72, No. 3, September 1978, pp. 996–1008; and Manus Midlarsky et al., "Why Violence Spreads: The Contagion of International Terrorism," *International Studies Quarterly,* Vol. 24, No. 2, June 1980, pp. 262–298.

[31] Or preemptive repression as we have noted above. See Danneman and Ritter, 2013.

[32] Eric M. Forman, "Civil War as a Source of International Violence," *Journal of Politics,* Vol. 34, No. 4, November 1972, pp. 1111–1134.

[33] See Bethany Lacina, "Explaining the Severity of Civil Wars," *Journal of Conflict Resolution,* Vol. 50, 2006, p. 276; and P. Collier and A. Hoeffler, *Greed and Grievance in Civil War,* World Bank Policy Research Working Paper 2355, World Bank, Washington, D.C., 2001; and Fearon and Laitin, 2003.

Timing/Ability/Effectiveness of Intervention. The specific timing and effectiveness of an intervention in an ongoing conflict will also determine the onset or severity of the conflict spillover. There are three main points of view: giving war a chance, negotiating a settlement, and arming opposition forces.[34] War advocates believe that letting war run its natural course is the most decisive solution for bringing about a form of peace. Negotiated settlement theorists suggest just the opposite. In fact, one source suggests that not intervening may lead to at least a 70-percent chance of a protracted conflict,[35] which may lead to spillover.[36] A third argument suggests that neither of these factors brings about lasting peace, but that improving security sector reform during the negotiation process may be far more beneficial than a simple cease-fire. The same argument holds that promises of intervention that do not materialize fare far worse than actual intervention itself because they create credibility issues internationally.[37]

Government and Insurgent Capabilities. The proficiency of the host state's military has a direct bearing on the potential for spillover. The capability and willingness of the host government to conduct operations may bring about a quick defeat of the opposition or may further prolong the conflict.[38] Further, the leader of the country in question may feel compelled to act to deter any further uprisings.[39]

---

[34] See Monica Duffy Toft, "Ending Civil Wars: A Case for Rebel Victory?" *International Security,* Vol. 34, No. 4, Spring 2010. pp. 7–36; and Edward N. Luttwak, "Give War a Chance," *Foreign Affairs,* Vol. 78, No. 4, July/August 1999, pp. 36–44. Also see debate between R. Licklider and R.H. Wagner in "The Consequences of Negotiated Settlements in Civil Wars, 1945–1993," *American Political Science Review,* Vol. 89, No. 3, September 1995.

[35] Beardsley, 2011.

[36] Beardsley also suggests that international intervention, especially with regard to securing porous borders, may actually inhibit insurgent movement and contain some of the effects of a conflict spillover.

[37] Toft, 2010.

[38] Halvard Buhaug, "Geography, Rebel Capability, and the Duration of Civil Conflict," *Journal of Conflict Resolution,* 2009, pp. 544–569.

[39] Barbara F. Walter, "Building Reputation: Why Governments Fight Some Separatists But Not Others," *American Journal of Political Science,* Vol. 50, No. 2, 2006, pp. 313–330. See also: Harvey Starr, "Opportunity and Willingness and the Nexus Between Internal and

The capability of rebels or opposition groups to supply, base, and carry out operations is crucial in assessing the likelihood of spillover. Research has shown that third-party or outside intervention becomes more likely when opposition or rebel groups are ethnically different from that of the aggressor, which is often the government. More capable opposition groups are more likely to have wider recruiting networks.[40] Intervention on the side of the opposition may further the legitimacy of the group, which can then attract more members and prolong the conflict. Spillovers in the form of refugee encampments provide fertile recruiting grounds once the legitimacy of their cause has been established.

External Conflict," paper prepared for presentation at the Annual Meeting of the Western Political Science Association, Seattle, March 20–23, 1991; and: Harvey Starr, " 'Opportunity' and 'Willingness' as Ordering Concepts in the Study of War," *International Interactions,* Vol. 4, 1978, pp. 363–387.

[40] Michael G. Findley, "Rethinking Third-Party Interventions into Civil Wars: An Actor-Centric Approach," *Journal of Politics,* Vol. 68, No. 4, November 2006, pp. 828–837.

CHAPTER THREE

Spillover of the Syrian Conflict into Turkey

Turkey has been and will continue to be significantly affected by the ongoing civil war in Syria. The enormous number of Syrian refugees alone will impose many financial and governance challenges. However, the prospects for the spillover of significant armed conflict into Turkey remain more limited. Turkey is a large, highly capable state with effective governing institutions and security services. The destabilization of the Turkish state itself due to the conflict that rages on its southern border is highly unlikely given current trends. For this reason, this case study will not include detailed discussions of the issues of fragility, perceived uncertainty, or access to open media that may have greater effects on other countries in the region.

Despite Turkey's overall resilience, a number of potential concerns remain. The vast refugee flows from Syria constitute a potential security threat if not managed properly. Syrian conflict may exacerbate existing ethnic and religious tensions within southern Turkey. Turkey has also effectively taken sides in Syria's civil war by supporting rebel groups, raising the possibility of direct military involvement in the conflict in

the future. Each of these potential sources of conflict spillover will be examined in greater detail.

External Support

Turkey has provided significant humanitarian, diplomatic, and even military support for Syrian rebel groups. Turkey serves as the transit route both for the majority of food aid that reaches rebel-controlled areas in northern Syria and for many foreign fighters that enter Syria to join with anti-Assad forces.[1] Turkey also provides tacit support to rebel military organizations, regularly allowing rebel fighters to cross the border for rest or to visit their families before returning to Syria to fight. Indeed, Turkey initially allowed the headquarters of the Free Syrian Army to operate from inside Turkey before the group relocated inside Syria in the fall of 2012.[2]

This direct support for anti-Assad groups runs the risk of involving Turkey more directly in the Syrian conflict. It makes Turkey a potential target for Syrian retaliation and increases the risk of localized conflict in Turkish border regions. Both possibilities will be assessed in greater detail.

Refugees

Turkey has thus far absorbed a tremendous number of refugees fleeing the Syrian conflict and been very generous in their treatment. Until 2013, most of these refugees were housed in well-run camps supported by the Turkish Red Crescent near the Turkey-Syria border. The current

---

[1]   Deborah Amos and David Greene, "How Food Aid Is Being Used As A Weapon In Syria," National Public Radio, July 29, 2013; Terry Atlas, "Foreign Fighters Flocking to Syria Stirs Terror Concerns," Bloomberg News, July 20, 2013.

[2]   Liam Stack, "In Slap at Syria, Turkey Shelters Anti-Assad Fighters," *New York Times,* October 27, 2011; Patrick McDonnell, "Free Syrian Army Will Shift Headquarters from Turkey to Syria," *Los Angeles Times,* September 23, 2012.

numbers housed in these tent or container camps exceed 200,000.[3] By all accounts, living conditions in these camps are comparatively high, and there have been few security issues.[4] Moreover, these camps are located far from most Turkish population centers, so the prospects for broader instability from the camps are limited. Turkey has received significant praise for its handling of this refugee population, particularly in the face of very limited international financial support for its operations.[5]

However, there are several signs that Turkey's capacity to manage these refugee flows in such a controlled manner has been exceeded. First, there has been a significant buildup of refugees inside Syria that Turkey has not allowed to cross the border because it lacks the space to house them effectively.[6] The construction of new camps is under way, but this buildup calls into question whether Turkey will be able to keep pace with future refugee flows or whether it will decide at some point to effectively close its border, with potentially stark consequences for those trapped on the other side.

Second, while conditions inside the camps generally far exceed those in comparable camps in other countries, they are nonetheless intended as short-term living arrangements. If the Syrian civil war were to stretch on for several years more, the refugee population could become dissatisfied with its economic and educational opportunities within the camp, and seek either relocation or integration into Turkish society, where effects on local populations would significantly increase.

Third, over the past year there has been a sharp increase in the number of Syrian refugees living in Turkey outside of the designated camps. Many refugees living outside the camps are

---

[3] United Nations High Commissioner for Refugees (UNHCR), "UNHCR Turkey Syrian Refugee Daily Sitrep," August 20, 2013.

[4] International Crisis Group, "Blurring the Borders: Syrian Spillover Risks for Turkey," Europe Report No. 225, April 30, 2013.

[5] Nisan Su Aras, "Turkey May Host 1 million Syrian Refugees by 2014," *Hurriyet Daily News,* June 21, 2013.

[6] Armin Rosen, "Turkey's Camps Can't Expand Fast Enough for All the New Syrian Refugees," *The Atlantic,* April 18, 2013.

concentrated in the southern Turkish provinces of Gaziantep and Hatay.[7] These refugees increase the pressure on the local economy and government to provide jobs, housing, and services and may as a result come into conflict with the local population.[8] Such conflict has been limited so far, although Syrian refugees were the targets of local anger in the aftermath of the May 2013 Reyhanli bombings, to be discussed in greater detail later.[9] If the concentration of Syrian refugees continues to increase, or the conflict in Syria persists for many years, Turkey may need to relocate refugees either to newly constructed camps or elsewhere in Turkey to avoid the possibility of localized conflict in suddenly overcrowded border areas.

Ethnic Ties

The ongoing civil war has the potential to increase conflict among groups within Turkey due to the complex ethnic and religious links that straddle the border. The two groups worthy of the greatest attention in this regard are Turkey's substantial Kurdish population throughout its southeast and its Arab Alevi minority concentrated in Hatay province.

The Turkey-Syria-Kurdish strategic triangle has been a significant source of conflict in the past. For many years, Syria supported the activities of the militant Kurdistan Worker's Party (PKK), allowing it to operate from Syrian territory and recruit from Syria's own sizable Kurdish minority in its campaign against the Turkish state throughout the 1980s and early 1990s.[10] In the late 1990s, however, in the midst of a general rapprochement between the two countries, Syria dropped its

---

[7] UNHCR, 2013. The potential for ethnic or religious conflict among Turkish citizens in Hatay will be discussed in more detail in the subsequent section.

[8] Constanze Letsch, "Syrian Refugee Crisis Raises Tensions in Turkish Border Towns," *The Guardian,* July 25, 2013.

[9] Kareem Fahim and Sebnem Arsu, "Car Bombings Kill Dozens in Center of Turkish Town Near the Syrian Border," *New York Times,* May 11, 2013.

[10] Jordi Tejel, "Syria's Kurds: Troubled Past, Uncertain Future," Carnegie Endowment for International Peace, October 16, 2012.

support for the PKK and began cooperating with Turkey on the prosecution of its members. In the early stages of the civil war in 2012, Syria withdrew its forces from its northern Kurdish areas, effectively ceding administration of the region to the Kurdish Democratic Union Party (PYD), an organization originally formed by Syrian Kurds returning from fighting alongside the PKK.[11]

The beginning of the Syrian civil war also coincided with a sustained attempt to finally settle the conflict between the PKK and the Turkish state. The PKK declared a cease-fire in March 2013 and has been engaged in negotiations with Ankara regarding greater autonomy for Kurdish areas in exchange for an end to the decades-long insurgency.[12] Turkish Prime Minister Recep Tayyip Erdogan has a strong incentive to see the deal completed, both due to the domestic political benefits of achieving peace and because it would strengthen Turkey's efforts to project its influence elsewhere in the region.[13] Turkey has pursued a series of economic agreements with Iraqi Kurdistan, which it sees as a potential source of much-needed energy resources.[14]

Turkey's improved relations with other Kurdish groups did not initially translate into a similar approach to the PYD, as Turkey feared that increased Kurdish autonomy within Syria would encourage secessionism.[15] The manner in which Syrian forces withdrew from the region may also have led Ankara to believe that the PYD was operating with the blessing of Damascus, concerns that appear to have been alleviated with the 2013 clashes between PYD and Syrian regime forces.[16]

---

[11] Tejel, 2012.

[12] Daren Butler, "Kurdish Militants in War of Words with Turkey Over Withdrawal." Reuters, August 19, 2013.

[13] Bayram Balci, "Turkish Protests, Syria Crisis Will Boost Turkey-PKK Peace Process," *World Politics Review,* July 29, 2013.

[14] Humeyra Pamuk, "Turkey Plays Big in Kurdistan's Energy Game," Reuters, August 15, 2013.

[15] Stephen F. Larrabee, "Is Turkey Rethinking the Syrian Kurd issue?" *CNN Global Public Square,* August 21, 2013.

[16] "PYD Begins Fight Against al-Assad Regime Forces in Northern Syria," *Hurriyet Daily News,* April 8, 2013.

In July 2013, Turkey invited the leader of the PYD, Saleh Muslim, to visit Ankara, where Muslim reaffirmed that his group did not intend to secede from Syria.[17] Turkey subsequently agreed to provide humanitarian aid to Kurdish areas in northern Syria, which had previously been withheld.[18]

Turkey's strong motivation to pursue constructive relations with Kurdish groups outside of Syria appears to have prevented any spillover of the civil war to Kurdish areas within Turkey and may even be facilitating a positive relationship between the Turkish and Syrian Kurdish groups. Although this dynamic certainly bears watching, the risk of the Syrian civil war inflaming the Kurdish conflict within Turkey appears to be low.

A potentially more contentious situation is the position of Turkey's Arab Alevi minority in Hatay province. Arab Alevis make up roughly a third of Hatay's population and differ from other groups in the province both in being Arabic speakers and in practicing an offshoot of Shi'ism similar (though not identical) to that of Syrian Alawites.[19] The group has long felt discriminated against by Turkish authorities. It is a strong supporter of Turkey's secular opposition party, the Republican People's Party, fearing the increasingly Sunni religious bent of the ruling Justice and Development Party.[20]

Arab Alevis share many links with the Syrian Alawite community, which forms the core of the Assad regime. The Arab Alevi community has thus been highly critical of Ankara's support of Syrian Sunni rebels, fearing that the increasingly sectarian nature of the conflict puts all minority Shi'a groups in the region at risk.[21] Arab Alevis

[17] Ben Hubbard and an NYT employee, "Kurdish Struggle Blurs Syria's Battle Lines," *New York Times,* August 1, 2013; Emine Kart, "Turkey Not Categorically Against Formation of Autonomous Kurdish Entity Inside Syria," *Hurriyet Daily News,* August 16, 2013.

[18] Kart, 2013.

[19] Soner Cagaptay, "Syria's War Could Inflame Turkey's Hatay Province," Washington Institute for Near East Policy, Policywatch 2063, April 4, 2013.

[20] Yavuz Baydar, "Bombing Exposes Divide in Turkish Politics," *al Monitor,* May 14, 2013.

[21] Jeffrey Gettleman, "As Syria War Roils, Unrest Among Sects Hits Turkey," *New York Times,* August 4, 2012.

have also been the subject of attacks by Syrian Sunni refugees, many of whom have suffered terribly at the hands of Alawite-dominated Syrian government forces.[22]

The Turkish government has sought to minimize these tensions by attempting to relocate many Syrian refugees in Hatay province elsewhere in Turkey.[23] However, with increasing refugee flows overall, the effectiveness of this effort is questionable—and if the civil war continues, the potential for some level of conflict between Arab Alevis and Syrian refugees in Hatay province seems high.

The potential for future conflict between Arab Alevis and the Turkish state also cannot be ignored, particularly if Ankara continues to cast its opposition to the Assad regime in sectarian terms and provide support to extremist jihadi groups in Syria. Nonviolent antigovernment Arab Alevi protests already occur with some regularity.[24] Such tensions would be unlikely to develop into an insurgency or other widespread, persistent conflict, but more limited incidences of localized violence against Turkish government interests remain plausible.

Timing/Effectiveness of Intervention

Turkey insists it has no interest in direct military intervention in the Syrian civil war.[25] Given the dire situation on the ground in Syria, and the fact that any country that did intervene militarily may find it difficult to extricate itself from the postwar situation, Turkey's statements are highly credible. Nonetheless, Turkey could intervene militarily in Syria in the context of a broader international action supported by either the United Nations or Turkey's NATO allies in Europe and the

---

[22] International Crisis Group, 2013. There do not, however, appear to be signs of significant tensions between Arab Alevis and other local groups in Hatay, where Sunnis and Alevis have lived in relative harmony for decades.

[23] Christopher Torchia and Mehmet Guzel, "Turkey Seeks to Relocate Some Syrian Refugees," Associated Press, September 16, 2012.

[24] Cagaptay, 2013.

[25] International Crisis Group, 2013, p. 30.

United States. The prospects for such an intervention are uncertain, if not unlikely. Russian opposition blocks any UN mandate for such a mission, and the Western appetite for direct involvement in the Syrian conflict appears to be limited regardless. However, in the event that these dynamics change in the future, perhaps due to atrocities against civilians committed by the Assad regime, Turkey would likely play a role in any intervention given its proximity, military capabilities, and strong relationships with outside powers.

Government and Insurgent Capabilities

The Syrian government could decide to attack Turkey in retaliation for Turkish support of rebel groups. Any significant invasion of Turkey by Syrian forces is, of course, implausible. However, smaller-scale attacks involving irregular or covert forces are possible and may already be occurring. The May 11th bombings in the Turkish border town of Rey-hanli killed more than 50 people, primarily Turkish citizens.[26] The Turkish government has linked the bombing to the Syrian regime, although Damascus denies any involvement.[27] The attack followed smaller bombings and mortar shelling in the same area over the previous several months.[28] Although these attacks have been relatively limited in nature thus far, a concerted retaliatory campaign by the Assad regime is possible and could prompt a more direct, military Turkish response. As for anti-Assad insurgent forces, although Turkey has been supportive of their efforts, these groups have not undertaken significant recruitment or other independent activities within Turkey. Any such developments would almost certainly be opposed by the Turkish state. The ethnic mixture near the Syria-Turkey border of Kurds and

---

[26] Erdem Güneş, "Death Toll Rises to 50 as Explosions Hit Turkish Town on Border with Syria," *Hurriyet Daily News,* May 11, 2013; "Reyhanli Bombings Death Toll Reaches 52," *Hurriyet Daily News,* May 27, 2013.

[27] Oren Dorell, "Turkey: 9 with Syrian Ties Arrested in Car Bombings," *USA Today,* May 12, 2013.

[28] "Blast Kills Dozens in Turkish Town Reyhanli on Syria Border," BBC News, May 11, 2013.

Alevis also limits the extent to which Sunni Syrian rebel groups could build their own operations inside Turkey.

Conclusions

Turkey faces significant challenges as a result of the devastating civil war that has consumed its southern neighbor, including the potential for direct intervention in Syria, a massive influx of refugees, and the possibility of increased tensions with its Arab Alevi minority. While the Turkish state is strong, and none of these challenges represents an existential threat, Turkey is likely to experience limited spillover of violent conflict from the Syrian civil war.

CHAPTER FOUR

Spillover of the Syrian Conflict into Lebanon

Conflict spillover from Syria into Lebanon is not a recent phenomenon. The civil war that began in 2011 in neighboring Syria has only exacerbated preexisting ideological, political, economic, and geographic issues that have plagued Lebanon for decades. Lebanon's particularly high risk of conflict spillover stems from its crippled government, division among its internal security forces, and continued external/Iranian support to Hizbollah. Leba-non remains the largest recipient of refugees from Syria yet has no official camps to host them. The influx of refugees has started to tip the sectarian balance within Lebanon, which has ignited historical hatreds between Sunni and Shia that have already cul-

minated in violence in the form of clashes along the Syrian border and bombings in Beirut. Lebanon's political parties are also heavily divided along pro-Syria and anti-Syria lines, which has led to political deadlock and a postponement of elections. Although Assad withdrew his military forces from Lebanon in 2005, Syria continues to heavily influence internal events within Lebanon.[1] As the Syrian opposition continues to battle supporters of Assad both in Syria and in Lebanon, the propensity for conflict to spill over further will remain high and drag Lebanon closer into what is quickly becoming a full-blown regional conflict.

External Support

Hizbollah remains one of the main antagonists preventing Lebanon from isolating itself from the current conflict in Syria. It has a history of enflaming sectarian tensions in the country. Drawing on support from Iran and Syria, it has polarized the political landscape within Lebanon.[2]

Iran's continued support of Hizbollah and the Assad regime has increased the flow of arms between Lebanon and Syria's northern borders. Reports suggest that Hizbollah, fearing a possible regime collapse in Syria, has moved many of its long-range missiles back into Lebanon to prevent the oppositions' access to them.[3] Conversely, the United States has increased aid to the Lebanese Armed Forces (LAF) in an attempt to quell the violence and combat illicit arms transfers.

External support to Hizbollah and its subsequent direct involvement in the Syrian conflict have brought it into direct conflict with Jabhat al-Nusra. This Sunni militant group, which has been linked to al-Qaida, is not only conducting a series of attacks against the Syrian

---

[1] This is due in part to U.N. Security Council Resolutions 1559 and 1680, and also to Lebanese civil pressure after the assassination of Rafik Hariri.

[2] Lebanon also sided with the March 8 Coalition, earning itself two seats within the cabinet of former Lebanon PM Miqati that it seeks to retain upon elections in 2014.

[3] See Rebecca A. Hopkins, *Lebanon and the Uprising in Syria: Issue for Congress*, Congressional Research Service, February 2, 2012, p. 9.

regime in support of the Free Syrian Army, but also has been targeting Hizbollah from within Lebanon's borders. The actions of Jabhat al-Nusra have also renewed the vigor of Lebanon's internal Sunni jihadist groups, which were not empowered to challenge the LAF or Hizbollah before.[4] This combination of events has fueled the rate at which the conflict is spreading into Lebanon and the region.

Refugees

The conflict in Syria and the resulting flow of refugees into Lebanon have proven detrimental to both nation states. Lebanon has borne much of the brunt of refugee outflow from Syria. Current registered UNHCR refugees are calculated at 1,069,723.[5] However, the actual number may be much closer to 1 million, with another million estimated by the end of 2014.[6]

The lack of a clearly defined border has facilitated the influx of refugees from Syria. U.N. Security Resolution 1680 had sought to remedy the border delineation issue after Syria's withdrawal in 2005, but no action was ever taken.[7] Many of Lebanon's main border checkpoints at Arida, Aboudieh, Ka'a, and Masna'a are located far from the internationally demarcated line and do not meet other international border norms.[8] Syrian refugees are crossing mainly through northern Lebanon but have also reportedly been crossing through east Lebanon via Baalbek.[9]

---

[4] Ana Maria Luca, "A Different Type of Spillover," *NOW,* April 19, 2013.

[5] See UNHCR, *Syria Regional Refugee Response,* web page, undated; "Rising Tide of Refugees," *Christian Science Monitor Weekly,* June 2, 2014, p. 2.

[6] This is an estimate from Lebanon's Interior Minister Marwan Charbel. "Charbel: Over 2 million Syrians in Lebanon by End Year!" *Middle East Times,* July 30, 2013.

[7] This may be due to the fact that the Lebanese simply have no incentive to do so, as many Lebanese feel "close" to ethnic groups within Syria.

[8] See NOW, *Lebanon-Syria Borders: 2009 Report,* undated.

[9] See *Too Close For Comfort: Syrians in Lebanon,* Crisis Group, Middle East Report, May 2013.

The absence of designated refugee encampments, coupled with Lebanese official statements that no camps will be constructed, further complicates the issue of spillover. Syrian refugees have been forced to assimilate by moving into preexisting structures in the poorest neighborhoods of Lebanon. While refugees have been welcomed in some areas, the influx of competing ideologies and new ethnic makeup (mainly among Sunni and Shi'ite groups) have begun to cause sporadic infighting. A direct spillover effect can be seen in Tripoli, between the predominantly Sunni neighborhood of Bab al-Tabbana and the majority Alawite neighborhood of Jabal Mohsen.[10] Friction between these two neighborhoods existed before the outbreak of the Syrian civil war,[11] with the Sunnis initiating skirmishes against Jabal Mohsen's Alawites.[12]

The influx of international aid to Syrian refugees arriving in Lebanon further affects much of Lebanon's indigenous populace, which had suffered long before Syria's current problems began. Preferential international treatment of Syria's refugees has begun to erode relations between refugees and their receiving groups in Lebanon. Resentful communities have begun to drive out recent settlers into regions of Lebanon where uneasy ethnic divisions already exist and may be prone to sectarian conflict.[13] Lebanese citizens must now also compete for wages with refugees who work for less. This has further strained relationships, as well as Lebanon's integration strategies.[14]

---

[10] Hala Naufal, "Syrian Refugees in Lebanon: the Humanitarian Approach Under Political Divisions," Migration Policy Centre, 2012/2013 Report, 2012.

[11] In 1986, prominent members of the Tawheed political movement in Bab al-Tabbana were massacred by the rival Alawi Arab Democratic Party backed by Syrian forces. Some suggest that the massacre still bears on the current conflict and that Suuni elements retain the memory of Syrian oppression, giving cause to an increase in conflict between pro- and anti-Syrian proponents. Also see: Serene Assir, "Tripoli Clashes: Keeping Conflict Alive," al-Akbhar, February 2012.

[12] Julie Taylor, "Leave Hezbollah Alone!" Foreign Policy, July 24, 2013.

[13] See Anne Barnard, "Swollen With Syrian Refugees, Lebanon Feels Its Stitching Fray," New York Times, February 23, 2013.

[14] Itani, 2013, p. 4.

Fragility of Neighboring States

Lebanon is a fragile state, politically, economically, and socially. Its geographic proximity to the Syrian conflict, and the preexisting tensions between ethnic and religious communities within its borders, have made it entirely vulnerable to violent spillover from Syria. The 375-kilometer geographical boundary that Lebanon shares with Syria has facilitated the travel of rebels, jihadists, and refugees, as well as the transfer of arms, money, and equipment.[15]

Before the outbreak of the civil war in Syria, the 2010 *Failed States Index* had placed Lebanon at 34 out of 60, while Syria was placed at 48.[16] As of 2013, the same index listed Lebanon at 46 and Syria at 21. The UN Development Program's 2013 Human Development Report further illustrates that Lebanon's growth has been stunted over the past two years.[17] While Lebanon may not show all of the hallmark signs of a fragile state,[18] the spillover effect from the conflict in Syria may cause it to go in that direction.

Lebanon's civil war from 1975–1990 and other sporadic conflicts since then have created a ripe environment for violence to spread. Existing security apparatuses—namely the LAF—were already stretched to the limit prior to the conflict and are vastly outmatched against Hizbollah. Moreover, the Taif agreement signed just before 1990 to bring an end to Lebanon's civil war does not appear to have quelled all of the tension and disagreement among Lebanon's various militia groups.[19]

Lebanon's civil war devastated an already aging infrastructure, which would now cost approximately $20 billion to overhaul to meet

---

[15] As opposed to a congruent geographical boundary with physical barriers, i.e. mountains, vast deserts, and oceans.

[16] For more on methodology, see foreignpolicy.com, *Failed States,* web page, undated.

[17] See UN Development Program, *Human Development Report 2013, The Rise of the South: Human Progress in a Diverse World,* undated.

[18] For example, as compared to Somalia, Congo, DRC, or Sudan.

[19] Patrick Galey, "Lebanon: Passing the Failed State Test," *al-Akhbar,* July 20, 2012.

current population demand.[20] Areas in northern Lebanon continue to provide ample supply routes for arms smuggling operations. Although Lebanon boasts a strong banking and tourism industry, the Lebanese government has had to borrow heavily to rebuild infrastructure— mainly in power and transportation sectors. International investment in Lebanon has also waned due to political instability. The influx of Syrian refugees has further exacerbated a weak educational system and created competition for low-wage employment.

The most important cause of fragility, however, is the Lebanese government itself. Following the Cedar Revolution in 2005, which came about as a result of the assassination of Rafiq Hariri, the political landscape of Lebanon was divided between pro- and anti-Syria proponents and other minority groups.[21] The majority Shia, pro-Assad group was dubbed the March 8 Coalition, while the majority Sunni, anti-Assad group became known as the March 14 Alliance as a result of the day that rallies were held in Martyr Square to protest the recent assassination. Nationalist resentment has grown as the majority Suuni refugee populace threatens to gain more representation in a plausible new government. Further, Lebanon's government remains in a "caretaker" status, which has been in effect since the resignation of Prime Minister Najib Miqati in March 2013, and elections have been postponed until November 2014. While the caretaker government in Lebanon theoretically retains the ability to govern and control state institutions, it has been unable to do so due to the lack of leadership and the political power vacuum created in the wake of Miqati's resignation, which has created friction among the various political groups.[22]

---

[20] Yara Bayoumy, "Lebanon Needs $20 Billion for Infrastructure," Reuters, October 20, 2010.

[21] The assassination was blamed heavily on Hizbollah and Syria forces.

[22] In addition, the International Security Forces are being managed by an interim director after the former leader retired. See Nour Samaha, "Is Lebanon Spiralling Out of Control?" al Jazeera, June 21, 2013.

Ethnic Ties

Ethnic groups within Lebanon share strong transnational and cultural ties with their respective Sunni, Shia, Druze, Christian, and Alawi counterparts in Syria. These relationships have been strained in recent months, but without these linkages, Syrian refugees would not be able to integrate into the social fabric as they have inside Lebanon.[23] The ethnic linkages are so strong that any action taken against one group in Syria has a direct impact on its related sect in Lebanon, and vice versa.[24] Although Lebanon has attempted to remain neutral in the conflict (abstaining from many of the Syrian sanction votes in the United Nations), it has been unable to do so because the country has become inexorably linked to action taken by the various groups in both countries.[25]

Access to Open Media

Since Lebanon is not governed by an authoritarian regime, freedom of the press and access to open media has, for the most part, remained unhindered during the current conflict. Nevertheless, reports have noted numerous unattributed attacks directed at outspoken journalists over the past decade.[26]

---

[23] However, Lebanon's state capacity to facilitate integration and enable safe havens has been called into question over the past year.

[24] For example, if the Free Syrian Army (FSA) conducts attacks within Lebanon, this prompts Shia groups to carry out attacks on Sunni groups. If Hizbollah conducts attacks within Syria, Al-Nusra (mainly Suuni) reciprocates the attacks.

[25] Lebanon can also be understood to have abstained from these votes since much of Lebanon's economy is dependent on land-based trade through Syria, in addition to shared banking operations between the two countries: "Syrian operations comprise 10 percent of consolidated balance sheets in Lebanese banks and Lebanese banks have loaned more than $1 billion to Syrian individuals and corporations." Hopkins, 2013, p. 8.

[26] See "Media in Lebanon: Reporting on a Nation Divided," IPI, December 2006; and Jad Melki et al., "Mapping Digital Media: Lebanon," Open Society Foundation, March 15, 2012

In 2009, a report noted that 66 percent of the Internet users in Lebanon were 15–29 years old, while only 18 percent were over 40.[27] While the notion of open media may have not played a direct role in facilitating conflict within Lebanon, it has contributed to the collective awareness and has made recruitment easier for opposition groups. This can be seen in the case of Fatah al-Islam and other Salafist groups within Lebanon that communicate with other insurgents through online jihadist forums.[28]

Perceived Uncertainty

The uncertainty of Hizbollah's future if the Assad regime falls has put the group in a difficult situation. Hizbollah has been Iran's conduit in Lebanon for more than 30 years, supplying weapons and finances via Syria. With its prime, overland, illegal trade route cut off, Hizbollah would have to seek new conduits for support from Iran. It is well established enough as a political actor and strong enough as a militia to survive within Lebanon.

After its 2006 war with Israel, Hizbollah was the political organization that repaired much of the infrastructure in the country—not the Lebanese government.[29] In recent years, however, the group has begun to face credibility issues because of its assault on Beirut in 2008.[30] Hizbollah targeting of opposition forces both in Syria and in Lebanon shows that the perceived threat of "losing" Syria to the FSA or Jabhat al-Nusra far outweighs any purely political risk at home. The threat of a Sunni Islamist government in Syria explains Hizbollah's willingness to engage in the fighting.

---

[27] See Target Group Index Lebanon, "Lebanon Internet Scene," 2009, market research report by Media Direction OMD, via OSF 2012 Report.

[28] Bilal Y. Saab, "The Syrian Spillover and Salafist Radicalization in Lebanon," *CTC Sentinel,* July 23, 2013.

[29] "With Syria In Shambles, the Uncertain Future of Hezbollah." NPR, February 26, 2013.

[30] Michael Totten, "The Beginning of the End for Hezbollah," *World Affairs,* April 22, 2013.

Government and Insurgent Capabilities

The LAF played a critical role after the 2005 pull-out of Syria from Lebanon and continues to represent a stabilizing force in the country. Despite recent efforts to balance sectarian divides within the LAF and strong support from nationalists, perceptions of the LAF—especially by the Sunni communities—have started to change for the worse in recent years.[31]

As noted earlier, the LAF is no match for Hizbollah. Its capabilities have been over-stretched in dealing with border incursions by Syrian opposition groups, assassinations, and kidnappings by various actors. The LAF in the past relied on the Syrian military for training and has collaborated numerous times with Syria against common enemies, which may suggest its semineutrality in the current conflict.[32] To date, it has primarily acted as a deterrent force within Lebanon rather than as a force capable of carrying out offensive, external military action. In the 2006 Israel-Hizbollah war, the LAF remained on the sidelines for the most part.

The United States has continued to support the LAF, which it sees as a stabilizing force in the region. However, the United States has also supported actions taken by the FSA. The LAF continues to deter or root out Syria's opposition forces (such as the FSA) within Lebanon; yet support to the FSA by the United States allows the group to develop basing options within Lebanon. External support in this instance has had the dual effect of complicating both LAF actions and FSA operations.

Sunni jihadist groups within Lebanon—such as Fatah al-Islam, Jund al-Sham, and the older Asbat al-Ansar—have been reinvigorated by the actions of their Sunni brethren in Syria. These insurgent groups in Lebanon had been kept in check by Hizbollah and by a relatively

---

[31] This is likely due to Sunni perceptions of the LAF letting Hizbollah have "free rein" while it heavily targets Syrian opposition groups in the region. Further, according to Nerguzian, 30 percent of the LAF's officer cadre is Shi'a. For more, see Aram Nerguzian, "The Lebanese Armed Forces: Challenges and Opportunities in Post-Syria Lebanon." CSIS, February 10, 2009.

[32] Nerguzian, 2009, p. 22.

unsupportive Lebanese Sunni community until the Syrian conflict began in 2011. Jabhat al-Nusra is also reported to be operating inside Lebanon, suggesting that Syrian refugee camps have been able to provide a base of operations to the Sunni jihadists, to a certain degree.[33] If Jabhat al-Nusra is not able to maintain a base of operations within Lebanon, it may be difficult for the older Salafist groups, such as al-Ansar, to remain effective. It is plausible that Jabhat al-Nusra could focus its fighting in Syria while directing Fatah al-Islam and Jund al-Sham from afar, though it would be difficult against a larger force such as Hizbollah.[34] Unless Jabhat al-Nusra is able to assimilate existing Lebanese groups into its core or achieve a series of major tactical successes in Lebanon, it probably will not significantly affect the ability of the state to carry out government functions.

Conclusions

The spillover of conflict from Syria into Lebanon is already in progress and might be irreversible unless the fighting inside Syria ends. The larger question is not how the spillover from Syria can be prevented, but what should be done now that it already has taken root? Lebanon's caretaker government is weak. The LAF remains internally divided on Syria's conflict. Refugees from Syria continue to flood into Lebanon thousands at a time, many not even registering for fear of retaliation. The FSA and other Syrian opposition groups, including Jabhat al-Nusra, continue to use Lebanon to strike back at Hizbollah. Syria itself launches attacks on opposition groups within Lebanese borders. External support from Iran to Hizbollah is sure to grow in the event of a U.S. strike on Syrian military targets. Most, if not all, of these issues will be difficult to tackle in the short term.

---

[33] "Lebanon Sentences al-Nusra Members to Death," *al-Alam,* July 19, 2013.

[34] See Saab, 2013.

CHAPTER FIVE

Spillover of the Syrian Conflict into Iraq

Several large Sunni Arab tribes inhabit both sides of the Iraqi-Syrian border. Trade, familial relations, and the smuggling of goods and people continued unabated during the greater part of the 20th century, even during times of political antagonism between the two leading branches of the Ba'ath Party, which was the leading political establishment in both countries. Even though a rift between Iraq and Syria from 1979 to the late 1990s pre-vented legal travel and trade between the two countries, the border region remained busy and accessible from both sides. Covert external intervention and the influx of for-eign fighters con-tinued to under-mine security in Iraq throughout the U.S. occupa-tion that started in 2003. Iraq's

borders with Syria and Iran were used as conduits through which fighters could cross. Safe havens were established inside these borders to provide logistical and technical support for various combatants in Iraq.

Today, the border remains porous, and these same tribal ties persist; however, Iraq's political and religious rifts are segregating people across the same sectarian lines that now define the main political agendas of combatants in Syria. Both Sunnis and Shia in Iraq have their eyes fixed with anticipation and strategic interest on how events might unfold in Syria. Both of these religious groups perceive the end state of the Syrian conflict as one that could play a major role in shaping Iraq's political future.[1]

External Support/Intervention

The security environment in Iraq has been unstable since the start of hostilities in Syria. A stream of low-level sectarian violence continued in 2013 to stoke hatred and increase chances of escalation throughout Iraq. Syrian opposition fighters that belong to groups affiliated with al-Qaida began establishing safe havens in western Iraq as platforms from which to launch their attacks inside the country in June 2014. Iraqi tribesmen—who see themselves obliged by tribal affiliation to help and who have an incentive to overthrow the Alawite Shia regime in Damascus—provided shelter and logistical support, and occasionally undertook joint operations within Iraq's borders. This became evident during several operations conducted to disrupt the outflow of weapon convoys from Iraq's central government to the Syrian regime in Anbar province.[2] These events were the first signs of spillover perpetrated by the Syrian opposition and its allies in Iraq—a spillover that has since turned into a full-scale invasion.

---

[1] These trends, as analyzed in 2013, became a reality in June 2014 when fighters from ISIS swept across the border and seized wide swaths of territory in the Sunni areas of northern Iraq.

[2] Duraid Adnan, "Massacre of Syrian Soldiers in Iraq Raises Risk of Widening Conflict," *New York Times*, March 4, 2013.

In addition, Iraqi Shia mosques *(husayniyas)* are openly recruiting fighters to help the Syrian regime against the rebels. These mosques are used as both recruiting and orientation offices for Shia fighters before they travel to Iran's Quds force training camps.[3] The not-so-secretive ceremonies that accompany the departure and return of these "Abbas Brigade" fighters have prompted attacks from Sunni insurgent groups in retribution for the killings of fellow Sunnis in Syria.[4] Unfortunately, the threat that these activities might broaden the conflict has not yet been addressed by the Iraqi government.

Refugees

Due to Iraq's highly fragile security environment and its own struggles with internally displaced populations, the country has been considered far from an ideal sanctuary for most families fleeing the violence in Syria. The Iraqi government, wary about the potential spillover of violence, at first attempted to block the inflow of Syrian refugees. The government later opened up its borders, after realizing that a 600-km desert is impossible to control and that a record of refugees coming in legally is preferable to losing track of them. Syrian refugees had, in fact, already made it to almost every city and town in the west and northwest of the country despite the initial prohibition against their entry.

The official numbers of registered Syrian refugees now exceeds 200,000.[5] Most of the unregistered refugees have been Sunni and Christian Syrians who fear that Iraq's Shia-dominated government will not

---

[3] Adam Shrek, "Iraqi Shiite Fighters' Role in Syria Grows More Prominent, Raising Sectarian Tensions at Home," Associated Press, June 10, 2013.

[4] Muna Mahmoud and Martin Chulov, "Syrian War Widens Sunni-Shia Schism as Foreign Jihadis Join Fight for Shrines," *The Guardian*, June 4, 2013.

[5] UNHCR, *Syria Regional Refugee Response*, undated. Since completion of this analysis in 2013, the overall refugee situation in Iraq has become even more complex as the result of the takeover of towns and territory north and west of Baghdad. Displaced Iraqis are estimated at 500,000 as of late June 2014—adding to the hundreds of thousands displaced earlier in the year. Tim Arango, "A Re-Ignited War Drives Iraqis Out in Huge Numbers," *New York Times*, June 29, 2014, p. 10

tolerate their existence. Those Sunni and Christian refugees who chose to first register (approximately 16,000 at the al-Qa'im Encampment for refugees in Anbar province), have had to put up with substandard living conditions in small encampments that are watched by Iraqi troops. Most other registered refugees in Anbar and Mosul have been kept in government buildings, schools, and other ad hoc facilities. The bulk of incoming refugees prior to June 2013 were still attempting to assimilate within the local population in small towns and villages, relying on savings, handouts, and daily employment opportunities as laborers.

The largest single wave of refugees crossing the border took place in late July and early August of 2013, shortly after Kurdish villages were attacked by the al-Qaida affiliate, Jabhat al-Nusra. The initial destinations of the most recent groups have been the northern cities of Irbil, Sulaymaniya and Dahuk. The Kurdish Regional Government (KRG) announced it received more than 50,000 refugees in a period of two weeks.[6] The KRG even opened several unofficial border-crossing checkpoints to facilitate the entry and settlement of refugees in the area.

The smuggling of jihadist fighters, weapons, and explosives through border villages was cloaked as part of the refugee flow.[7] The sharp increase in violence in Iraq during the summer of 2013 and thereafter was likely an outcome of increased operational capacity and the convergence of objectives of the two branches of al-Qaida in Syria and Iraq, despite their growing political differences and animosity. The vulnerability of refugees in Iraq has added significantly to the pool from which al-Qaida is recruiting, increasing the fear that radicalized Sunni youth in the Kurdish areas will join their ranks. The grievances caused by some Iraqi government policies are encouraging locals to join these groups as they gain in significance and momentum. There were reports in 2013 that al-Qaida in Iraq had actually shifted its main base of operations into Syria and had begun using Iraqi territories to set up safe havens and support stations that they could rely on when needed.[8]

---

[6] "UN Aid for Refugees in Syria, Iraqi Kurdistan," *al-Jazeera* (Arabic), August 27, 2013.

[7] "Time Explains: How Syria's War is Reviving Al Qaeda in Iraq," Time, undated.

[8] Margret Brennan, "Al Qaeda in Iraq Has Shifted Base of Operations to Syria, State Dept. Says," CBS News, August 13, 2013.

Another aspect of the spillover into Iraq has been the fighting between the Kurds and Jabhat al-Nusra in northeastern Syria and the large number of Kurdish refugees pouring across the border. The KRG was initially accused of aiding Syrian rebels and is now allegedly training and arming some of the Syrian and Kurdish refugees in Northern Iraq[9]—and allowing some to go back into Syria to carry on fighting.[10] A large number of these Kurdish refugees have joined forces with the local Kurdish militia (Peshmurga). Iraq's central government in Baghdad, as well as some of the major Arab tribes bordering Iraqi Kurdistan, has been worried that increased Peshmurga numbers and capability could lead to a land-grab attempt by Kurdish leaders. Insurgent groups like the al-Naqshabandiya army in Iraq might feel compelled to act against the Kurds if such threats are realized.[11] The operations might be sanctioned by Baghdad if the Kurds attempt to seize Kirkuk.[12]

Fragility of Neighboring States

Repercussions from the social mistrust, the failed economy, and the implications of a severely weakened security apparatus (which was later disbanded)[13] surfaced after the 2003 invasion. In the years that followed, Iraq spiraled into an almost all-out civil war that killed no fewer than 3,000 people per month at its peak.[14] Ethnically mixed and

---

[9] Henry Adams, "BACKGROUND: Iraqi Kurdistan Backing Syrian Rebels While Baghdad Supports Assad Online," United for Peace of Pierce County website, December 28, 2012.

[10] World Security Network, "Syrian Kurds Given Military Training In Northern Iraq, Says Barzani," October 25, 2012.

[11] Al-Naqshabandi Army is the main Sunni insurgent group in North-Central Iraq. These are tribal forces with a religious overtone, but they are not affiliated with Al-Qaida.

[12] ISIS's seizure of territory across northern and western Iraq in June 2014 has opened the door further for the Kurds to take complete control of their areas and protect themselves and their wider economic interests from the civil war developing between Sunni and Shia.

[13] Coalition Provisional Authority, Order 51, Suspension of Exclusive Agency Status of Iraqi State Company for Water Transportation, May 16, 2003.

[14] Hannah Fischer, *Iraqi Civilian Death Estimates,* Congressional Research Service, RS22537, August 27, 2008.

religiously mixed neighborhoods all but disappeared from Iraq's main cities. The country ranks 11th in the failed state index.[15] Corruption remains a rampant problem that undermines the country's ability to rebuild its devastated infrastructure, education, and public service sectors. In 2012, Transparency International ranked Iraq as low as 169th out of 174 total countries studied.[16] The country is home to a large number of armed militias, insurgent groups, religiously motivated terrorist organizations, and neighboring countries' proxy fighters. Iraq today remains one of the most dangerous, violent, and fragile countries in the world.[17]

On top of all this, Sunni and Shia populations are increasingly aligning with the two combating parties in Syria, and against each other. In 2013, Sunnis began allowing Syrian fighters to nest within their communities as refugees, and Shia were increasingly involved in the fight against Syrian rebels in Syria at that time. The political impasse created by Nuri al-Maliki's government in Baghdad and its marginalization of its Sunni participants caused most Sunni cabinet members to resign. The perception of legal system abuse that was seen by Sunnis as a political ethnic cleansing tool reached its apex when the highest-ranking Sunni politician, Iraqi Vice President Tariq al-Hashimi, was sentenced to death in absentia. Shia and Sunnis have been locked in a race to gather weapons and ammunition for a war seen as growing more inevitable every day.[18] The Shia-dominated government in Baghdad is afraid of the return of Sunni domination if the rebels in Syria emerge as winners, while Sunnis think the only hope of strengthening their hand in government is by ensuring the rebels' victory in Syria.[19]

---

[15] foreignpolicy.com, undated.

[16] Transparency International, *Corruption Perceptions Index,* country results, undated.

[17] Sara Gates, "Human Rights Risk Atlas 2013: Maplecroft Releases Annual Ranking Of Countries At Risk Of Human Rights Violations," Huffington Post, December 13, 2012.

[18] These developments became a reality in June 2014, as fighting erupted between Islamic militants in ISIS and the Shia regime of al-Maliki in Baghdad. What appears to be growing into a full civil war shows no signs of abating.

[19] Tim Arango, "Syrian War's Spillover Threatens a Fragile Iraq," *New York Times,* September 24, 2012.

Ethnic Linkages/Cultural Ties

There are a number of important religious, tribal, and ethnic connections between the Iraqi and Syrian people. In cities like Dayr al-Zur and Qamishli, family units are literally split between the two countries. Residents of towns in western and northwestern Iraq such as Anna, Rawa, Hayt, and Haditha all have direct tribal and ethnic affiliations with Syrians in the Albu–Kamal and Dayr al-Zur areas while Kurds in Mosul and Dahuk have relatives who live in Qamishli. Marriages within these families often took place across the two countries' borders with difficulty during the 1980s and early 1990s, but strong ties were renewed after the Iraq war in 2003, when large numbers of Iraqi refugees fled Iraq to Syria. These newly formed familial relationships are now working as a catalyst to help Syrian refugees assimilate within Iraqi society.

If the Syrian rebels were able to depose Assad, the next Syrian government might be a Sunni one. A Sunni-led government in Syria would give the large Sunni province in al-Anbar a better chance of succeeding politically and economically.

The Iraqi Shia community, on the other hand, is invested in ensuring that the Assad regime emerges intact in Syria. It is afraid that Sunni Iraqis might be emboldened by any success achieved by their counterparts in Syria and is trying to deny such leverage. Large numbers of fighters are encouraged to participate in Assad's campaign against the rebels, and these fighters receive funding and logistical support by the entire network of Shia-managed mosques in Iraq.

Tensions in Iraq will continue to rise as long as conflict continues in Syria. It could lead those competing for power in Iraq to take up arms against each other. A prompt settlement in Syria, regardless of the winner, could help improve the climate for Iraqis to negotiate an end to their differences. A continuation of the conflict, however, is likely to continue adding fuel to the civil conflict in both countries.[20]

---

[20] This trend is increasing, as sectarian fighting approaches civil war proportions in June 2014, pitting Sunni against Shia and ISIS jihadists against al-Maliki's government in Baghdad.

Access to Technology/Open Media

Iraq has one of the lowest rates of Internet use in the region: 7.1 per 100 people. This figure compares poorly with neighboring countries like Jordan (41/100), Saudi Arabia (54/100), and Egypt (44/100).[21] The infrastructure required for increasing Internet access is absent, as is any private or public funding to do so in the near future. Moreover, the government-provided dial-up system is primitive and heavily monitored, excluding it as a source of reliable and unbiased information.

The major source of information in Iraq is satellite TV, and most of these channels are funded by the Saudis, Qataris, and Iranians. Arabic-satellite channels usually attempt to bring in an audience for the Syrian opposition that takes its side of the conflict, while Iranian-sponsored channels do exactly the opposite. Despite being one of the most dangerous countries for journalists, Iraq has abundant print media.[22] However, the quality and objectivity of these papers are far below international standards, and the heavy-handed persecution of government opponents has reduced these publications to the level of local tabloids.

The absence of objective media sources and mistrust of local media in general have made Iraqis susceptible to rumors, word-of-mouth news, and organized political information campaigns. This is particularly dangerous, given the ease with which public opinion can be influenced. Religious propaganda, which uses the mosque and husayniyah as launching platforms, has a profound role in shaping public responses to the conflict in Syria, a conflict that has turned into a religious war along the same fault lines of Iraq's.

---

[21] World Bank, *World Development Indicators,* 2012.

[22] Ariel Zirulnick, "The Five Most Dangerous Countries for Journalists," *Christian Science Monitor,* undated.

Government and Insurgent Capabilities

Iraq spends more than 5 percent of its GDP on its military alone,[23] and spends almost the same amount on its police and other kinds of security organizations. It has 191,000 volunteer soldiers, 450,000 policemen, 192 main battle tanks, and a similar number of armored personnel carriers.[24] The government of Iraq is seeking to expand its military power rapidly, mostly aiming at bolstering its air force firepower. However, the main expansion is noted within the ground forces. The number of infantry divisions has grown from 13 to 16 in the last two years, with only one armored division. The nature of expansion is likely aimed at combating internal threats rather than defending the country against foreign aggression. There appears to be little effort devoted to stopping the flow of weapons, fighters, equipment, and money crossing between Iraq and Syria, whose government is completely unable—and in some cases unwilling—to stop the flow of cross-border traffic. There also has been little effort to develop unit cohesion and morale.

The strength of Sunni fighters in Iraq is in their commitment and number, which is in the tens of thousands. The fighters are mostly Nationalists, Salafists, and former Ba'athists, with some additional tribal fighters. A small fringe element of these fighters is associated with the Iraqi branch of al-Qaida and its affiliated organization, ISIS, which is now in open conflict with its co-religionists in al-Qaida and Jabhat al-Nusra. The precise number of fighters in this group is unknown and could fluctuate from time to time. Since the withdrawal of American troops from Iraq and the increasing marginalization of Sunnis in the Iraqi government, the boundary between al-Qaida in Iraq (AQI) and the rest of the Sunni fighting groups has become more ambiguous. Individuals who abandoned AQI during the U.S. troop surge have resumed their support.[25]

---

[23] World Bank, 2012.

[24] "Factbox: Iraq's Military Strength," Reuters, December 11, 2011.

[25] As of June 2014, Sunni jihadists are coalescing under the banner of ISIS in what appears to be the beginning of a civil war that has already led to the de facto partitioning of the country.

Despite its limited numbers, AQI remains a strong player in Mosul, the Iraqi Jazira area, and Rabi'a in Northern Iraq. The major tribes in these areas (mostly in Nineveh province) did not participate actively in the U.S.-sponsored tribal awakening movement in 2007 and 2008.[26]

The number of fighters in Jabhat al-Nusra is better established. The Al-Jazeera news service puts the total number of al-Nusra at 4,000.[27] Another source puts it at 7,000.[28] Recent estimates put the number of foreign fighters alone at 4,000, and the total number of fighters, including those from Syria, at more than 12,000.[29] According to a report by al-Jazeera,[30] the majority of fighters are Syrians, and recruitment is growing rapidly. Foreign fighters in a descending order according to their numbers are Saudis, Tunisians, Jordanians, and Iraqis. Most Jordanian fighters are spread out in the south near Dar'a and Damascus, while Iraqi and Saudi fighters are mostly found in Hums, Hama, and western provinces. Iraqi fighters are not members of al-Nusra, but rather from AQI. This has created fissures between the two groups over issues such as chain of command and local leadership.[31] The strength of these groups is growing across both sides of the Iraqi–Syrian border, and the tactics used by al-Nusra and AQI guarantee a strong role in shaping the strategy of the Syrian opposition. It is most likely that such influence will continue to grow as long as the conflict continues in Syria.

---

[26] This undoubtedly played a key role in ISIS's ability to take control of Mosul so quickly in June 2014.

[27] Mohammad Al-Najar, "Al-Nusra in Syria Learned From Lessons Passed," *al-Jazeera* (Arabic source), May 2013.

[28] "Syria's Islamist Fighters: Competition Among Islamists," *The Economist,* July 20, 2013.

[29] Mohammad Al-Najar, "Syrian Front 'Melts' in Anticipation of US Strike," *al-Jazeera* (Arabic source), September 2013; syrftr.com, "Syria the Future, A Jordanian Salafi Leader Estimates Al-Nusra Fighters at 12,000," April 2013.

[30] Al-Najar, May 2013.

[31] Arabic Sky News, "A Dispute over Integrating Al-Nusra Front to AQI," June 2013.

Conclusions

Syrian and Iraqi social structures are intertwined—the two countries share similar elements of instability, long and porous borders, and tribal connections, and they are both considered focal points of religious rivalry in the region. Numerous fighters from both sides have already taken part in the fighting both against and with the Syrian regime. Sunni tribes perceive a potential victory as an advantage in their own political struggle against the Shia religious political parties in power in Baghdad. On the other hand, the Shia-led Iraqi government is keen to deny its adversaries any advantages in the ongoing power grab being played out in Iraq. Competition between Iraq's Sunni and Shia communities is made worse by the spillover of violence from Syria. Already pitted against each other in a contest for power in post-Saddam Iraq, the two communities now find themselves on opposite sides in a brutal civil war next door—and one that is beginning at home.

CHAPTER SIX

Spillover of the Syrian Conflict into Jordan

The conflict in Syria between Assad's forces and the rebel opposition is already wearing on the delicate political, economic, and social fabric of Jordan. The potential for violence from the civil war in Syria spreading inside Jordan is high despite the capabilities of its security services. The growing refugee population along the border puts excessive pressure on already scarce water supplies and a civilian and security infrastructure that cannot bear the weight.[1] The radicalization of Syrian youth in Jordanian refu-

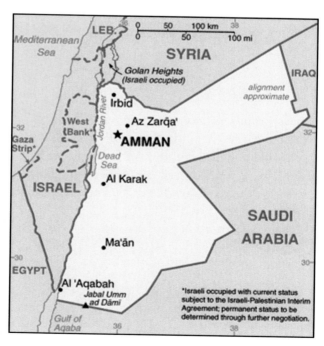

---

[1] For a good assessment of the refugee problem in Jordan, see David Remnick, "Letter from Jordan: City of the Lost," *New Yorker*, August 26, 2013, pp. 49–57; and Michael Gerson, "The Reluctant Refuge," *Washington Post*, August 23, 2013, p. A19.

gee camps and the breadth of reach these extremist ideas can have on the more radical elements of the Jordanian population in areas such as Ma'an, however, are the primary causes for concern. Over time, the frustration and deteriorating conditions within the refugee camps—along with the continued killing of civilians in Syria—will harden attitudes across the region and facilitate the recruitment efforts of al-Qaida and its jihadist affiliates inside Jordan. It seems equally likely that these more radical Sunni elements will come into direct contact with their Shia counterparts, who live among the hundreds of thousands of Iraqi Shia still in Jordan from the First and Second Gulf Wars. The likely presence of Iranian operatives in Amman and other Jordanian cities also bears watching, in light of the role Hamas may choose to play in the region as it develops its relationship with al-Qaida in Gaza and Sinai.[2] Jordan's role as a platform for assisting the flow of weapons and money from the Arab Gulf into Syria could lead to armed retribution as it has between Hizbollah and Sunni jihadists in Lebanon.[3]

External Support

Money, weapons, and fighters moving through Jordan into Syria will increase the level of fighting in Syria rather than decrease it. This means more civilians will die and more refugees will enter Jordan and other neighboring states. Jordan's continued association as an entry point of support for the rebels in the conflict means that some of the weapons, money, and fighters will pass back into Jordanian society through the very same black market mechanisms and smuggling routes used to aid the rebels. Jordan will be blamed by both sides and retributive actions

---

[2] For additional information on this issue see Robert Worth, "Lawless Sinai Shows Risks Rising in Fractured Egypt," *New York Times,* August 11, 2013, p. A1; Anthony Cordesman, *Iran's Revolutionary Guards, the Al-Quds Force, and Other Intelligence and Paramilitary Forces,* Center for Strategic and International Studies, August 16, 2007, p. 9.

[3] For additional information on these topics, see Ben Hubbard and Hwaida Saad, "Deadly Blast Rocks a Hizbollah Stronghold in Lebanon," *New York Times,* August 16, 2013, p. A4; and Loveday Morris and Suzan Haidamous, "Bomb Kills at Least 18 in Beirut," *Washington Post,* August 16, 2013, p. A8.

An aerial view shows the Zaatari refugee camp on July 18, 2013, near the Jordanian city of Mafraq, some eight kilometers from the Jordanian-Syrian border.
SOURCE: AFP/Mandel Ngan/Getty

will be taken against the Jordanian government and society at large. As of June 2014, support was growing for The Islamic State declared by ISIS in Iraq and Syria.[4] The chaos inside Syria and the criminal elements involved in the illicit trade along the border form a toxic mix that can only contribute further to the instability. Halting this cross-border flow as part of a larger international effort to create safe zones within Syria would be one way to impede the spillover. The contagions of refugee flow and external military assistance would also be contained as trafficking would be curtailed and refugees could be moved back into protected areas on the Syrian side of the border. Jordan could reap benefits by playing a key role in the humanitarian effort.

Refugees

The pervasive presence of Syrian refugees in Jordan poses the greatest threat to the country's stability—set at 593,346 in June 2014 in

---

[4]   William Booth and Taylor Luck, "In Jordan, Concern Over the Allure of ISIS," *Washington Post,* June 29, 2014, p. A14.

the Zaatari refugee camp inside the northern border, with plans to establish a second camp in Azraq, and an estimated two million more Syrians throughout the rest of Jordan.[5] It is difficult not to see refugee camps like Zaatari transforming themselves over time into small towns similar to the ones in Jordan today that were set up as Palestinian refugee camps after the wars with Israel. Many refugees, because they blend in so well culturally and linguistically, have entered Jordanian society directly. The poorer ones can be found squatting along some of the main roads while others with money have opened small restaurants and other competitive businesses in the major cities. Even though the Jordanian government and the Free Syrian Army have reduced the flow of refugees from as many as 5,000 a day to a more controlled trickle,[6] their continued presence and ability to blend into Jordanian society increases the prospect for the infection of radicalism from the civil war to spread: There will continue to be a pool of disaffected youth from which al-Qaida and other religious extremists can recruit, and both the anger and radical ideology resident in the refugee camps will work their way through Jordanian society as a whole. To diminish the likelihood of violence from the Syrian civil war spilling over into Jordan, it would be best to develop a way to safeguard the returning refugees and protect them against reprisals and genocide from both sides in the conflict. Doing so would limit the influence of many of the more extremist elements among the refugees and would remove them geographically as a physical threat to the rest of the Jordanian population. Returning the refugees without placing them directly in harm's way, however, is likely to require a negotiated cease-fire and some form of commitment to provide for their security under the mandate of an international stabilization force, and perhaps a no-fly zone in Syria similar to the one in Northern Iraq in the mid-to-late 1990s.

---

[5] UNHCR, *Syria Regional Refugee Response,* undated.

[6] Michael Gerson, "War's Exacting Toll," *Washington Post,* August 27, 2013, p. A17.

Fragility

Jordan is stable but fragile. King Abdallah's position is not as sure-footed as his father's was. He walks a fine line between support from the Palestinian Jordanians, who are the majority of the population (perhaps as high as 70 percent), and the native Bedouin and other tribes. These "East Bankers," who for generations have formed the bedrock of Jordanian society, compose the bulk of Jordan's security services and military, and are the ones the Hashemite monarchy has relied on for its survival.[7] In addition to the uncertainty bred by the slow shift in the country's political demographics away from the traditional tribal sources of support for the monarchy toward the majority of Palestinians (whose queen is Palestinian by birth and whose son will be king someday), there is continued uncertainty about the country's economy, which suffers from a severe drop in tourism revenues and a continued lack of significant revenue from indigenous industry. On top of all of this, the man on the street now openly criticizes the king and queen for their lavish lifestyle. The fact that the criticism is open shows the strength of the monarchy's commitment to democracy but also underscores the rising level of discontent and the fragile nature of the state at the moment. The obligation to cope with an influx of radicalized youth and the burdens of an overflow of refugees from the fighting in Syria will not help Jordan.[8] To impede the spillover of violence, the United States, the Arab Gulf, and the world community may need to shore up Jordan's economy using all practical means. Leaving the country to fend for itself will make it vulnerable, jeopardizing its stability and decreasing its effectiveness both as a close ally for the United States and as a buffer between the jihadists in Syria and the Arab Gulf.

---

[7] For an excellent discussion of these issues, see William Booth, "Jordan Keeping a Wary Eye on Israeli-Palestinian Talks," *Washington Post,* February 14, 2014, p. 8.

[8] For further analysis of this general phenomenon, see Salehyan and Gleditsch, 2006; and Fred Pearce, "Youthquake," *New Scientist,* July 20, 2013, pp. 42–45.

Ethnic Ties

In addition to the usual family ties between those who live and work in the borders areas of the Middle East, there is a natural cultural affinity between the Jordanians and the Syrians, and the people of the Levant as a whole. They share a common culture and speak the same Arabic. The predominantly Arab al-Qaida is at home here, unlike in Somalia, Afghanistan, and Mali. Jordan and Syria are central to the Arab world. This centrality gives the extremists ready access to the populations they found more aloof in other parts of the Middle East, South Asia, and Africa. The divide between Sunni and Shia, coupled with the ugliness of civil war, makes the ethnic-religious mix potentially explosive. Both sides in the Syrian civil war view the fight as zero-sum and as key to their continued existence. The external players in Iran and the Arab Gulf, who are fueling the fight, view the conflict the same way. It is not hard to see how this can spill into Jordan and further complicate the Jordanian political and social landscape. For example, the large number of Iraqi, Lebanese, and now Syrian Shia inside Jordan are likely to sympathize with their brethren in Damascus and in Shia enclaves along the Syrian coast. Some may take part by crossing the border and joining the fight; others could take part by continuing the struggle in the Jordanian cities where they now reside. Keeping the fight in Syria by means of strengthening the economy and improving the certainty of life at home in Jordan is one of the better ways to contain, if not reverse, the trend toward greater local involvement in the broader regional conflict.

Access to Open Media

An open society is vulnerable if it is fragile. Jordan is both open and fragile: open to social media and fragile in the many ways already noted. Everyone in Jordan has access to social media outlets and can use them to spread their views. In turn, the government can monitor these communications and apply any number of new predictive analytics to the social media feeds for early warning indications of social unrest. Access to these technologies in Jordan can certainly help terrorists and others mobilize large numbers of people quickly, but they are not likely to tip the scales in terms of destabilizing the country. In fact, social media is equally useful as a tool for the government and other social groups to garner support, combat the jihadist message directly, and shape the way the Syrian issue is perceived in general. Using social media in this way could actually help impede the spread of violence in the country.

Perceived Uncertainty

The Jordanian government and society at large have not yet reached the level of uncertainty that would prompt a political and military overreaction to the Syrian civil war. The cultural and linguistic affinities between the Syrians and the Jordanians have allowed the refugees from the conflict to be easily accepted into Jordanian society, and the Jordanian military has restrained itself from incursions into Syrian territory. This bodes well for the future if the conflict persists for years and the refugees become a permanent part of the social fabric of Jordan. That possibility alone, however, increases the risk of gradual wear and tear on the country's already struggling economy and infrastructure. If the war continues indefinitely as the result of a stalemate, then the degree of uncertainty and the pressure on the attitudes of the people may lead to resentment and oblige the Jordanian government to take measures to abruptly stop the influx of Syrian refugees and restrict government benefits for those already in Jordan. This type of resentment and government action (and perhaps overreaction) could play into the hands of the extremists on both sides of the fight and on both sides of the border.

Timing/Effectiveness of Intervention

The world community's delay in intervening to stop the civil war in Syria when it began has increased the power and broadened the influence of Hizbollah and Sunni jihadists in the region. Their positions in the eyes of their respective communities as victors, heroes, and saviors will make it hard to turn public perceptions against them and change the direction of the conflict—two necessary steps in preventing the spread of violence into Jordan and neighboring states. Limited measures, such as continuing to arm both sides, are likely to do little to stop the conflict, which is one of the keys to reversing the potential for spillover.

The result has been the creation a vacuum in which Sunni jihadists and Hizbollah can operate, winning over portions of the population in Syria by providing social welfare services and consolidating their territorial gains, such as in almost all of eastern Syria around the town of Raqqah and along the Euphrates River. Acknowledging that this has occurred and accepting the reality that Syria is no longer one state may enable the United States and its allies in Europe and the Middle East to deal with the threats more effectively and negotiate a way to prevent the conflict from spreading into Jordan and throughout the rest of the region. Early intervention to stop the conflict in Syria could have prevented this from happening—and would have better safeguarded a key U.S. ally in the region from the potential dangers posed by the spreading conflict.

Government and Insurgent Capabilities

The Syrian government and its armed forces are unable and unwilling to prevent the spread of conflict beyond their borders. Broadening the conflict has actually served their interests by drawing in support from Iran, Russia, and Hizbollah, and by keeping Israel uncertain and hesitant. Jordan, a longtime rival of the regime in Damascus, cannot count on any help in controlling the border areas between their countries or the spillover of violence from the civil war. The insurgents, on the other hand, are in an ideal position to spread their ideologies and extend their reach into Jordan and surrounding states by using the pipelines set up to hasten the arrival of foreign fighters, the refugee camps as recruiting grounds, and the smuggling and financial networks that are feeding the war. Each side in the conflict has a presence in Jordan and can draw on and spread influence throughout the Sunni and Shia communities there. The key question is: At what point will these groups move to incite violence that will begin to unravel the social fabric in Jordan by pitting Sunni against Shia, and at what point will these groups begin to take action in retribution against the Jordanian government for its role in supporting the rebels in Syria?

Conclusions

The potential for violent conflict from the civil war in Syria spreading into Jordan is relatively high. All of the key factors leading to spillover point in this direction. Primary among these factors is that, as a transit point for external support to the rebels, Jordan opens itself up to retribution from Hizbollah, Iran's Quds Force, and other agents of the regime in Damascus. Attacks against Jordanian government and Sunni civilian targets inside Jordan could make the country a secondary battlefield for jihad and force the Jordanian security services to use extreme measures to maintain order—a move that could make matters worse. A large and disaffected but easily amalgamated refugee population along the border and throughout Jordanian society would make it easy for jihadists to further their cause (i.e., radicalizing and recruiting Jordanian youth) and destabilize the state. The smuggling networks and manageable terrain within the region ensure equal access into Jordan for each side in the conflict through Syria, Iraq, Saudi Arabia, Lebanon, Palestine, and Egypt. The network linkages between these areas are significant. Finding ways for Jordan to contain or return the refugees to Syrian territory and to ease out of its role as a transit point for external support to the rebel factions in Syria would go a long way to curbing the potential for the spillover of violence from the war next door.

CHAPTER SEVEN

Conclusions and Recommendations

All of the factors leading to the spread of violent conflict from civil war and insurgency are present in the Levant. There is a high probability that the fighting in Syria, if left unchecked, will spill over into Turkey and Jordan, where both countries are engaged in providing external aid to the rebels and where both are serving as hosts to serious numbers of refugees with ethnic ties to their own populations.[1] Jordan is especially vulnerable because of its fragile economic condition and the potential political impact of demographic changes within its society. Violence has already spread into Lebanon because of the support Hizbollah is giving to the Assad regime in Damascus and is exacerbating the ever-present and complicated sectarian violence between Sunni and Shia in Iraq as fighters from ISIS claim territory in the west and establish a new Islamic state.[2] The strengthening of militant groups like al-Qaida and Jabhat al-Nusra in the border areas inside eastern Syria and western Iraq does not bode well for the stability of Baghdad or the region, which is best viewed as an extended part of an interconnected, dynamic whole and as a perceived battle for survival between Sunni and Shia—as well as an opportunity for either side to attack Israel.[3]

---

[1] William Booth and Loveday Morris, "Alleged Chemical Attack Leaves One Family Reeling," *Washington Post,* August 26, 2013.

[2] Loveday Morris and Ahmed Ramadan, "Blasts Kill at Least 27 in Lebanon," *Washington Post,* August 24, 2013, p. A1; Liz Sly and Loveday Morris, "Militants Announce Creation of a Formal Islamic State," *Washington Post,* June 30, 2014, p. A6.

[3] William Booth, "Group Linked to al-Qaida Claims Rocket Attack on Israel," *Washington Post,* August 23, 2013, p. A11.

The tight geography of the region, where everyone is in close proximity, makes spillover easier and more likely.[4] The declaration of a new Islamic state by ISIS militants in eastern Syria and western Iraq in late June 2014 brings them ever closer, and increases the potential for tearing away at the fabric of Jordanian society.

Lessons from the literature and from an analysis of the factors at play in the Levant suggest that to avoid spillover, it is necessary to

- intervene early and either negotiate or impose a settlement to prevent civilian casualties and the creation of refugee populations that inevitably lead to a hardening of positions and an intensification of conflict
- work with allies and neighboring states to stem the flow of foreign fighters and external aid
- work with allies and neighboring states to prevent the influx of refugees and to provide safe zones for their return
- provide military and financial assistance where needed to secure borders and inoculate the neighboring state populations and governments from the instability that comes from the spread of radical ideologies, economic hardships, and war.

To impede the spillover of violence now occurring in Lebanon and Iraq and to reverse the likelihood of it spreading into Turkey and Jordan, it will be necessary to address the underlying causes of the spillover in the region by

- negotiating with and persuading the Arab Gulf states, Iran, and Russia to curtail their military assistance to the rebels and the regime
- negotiating or imposing a cease-fire to permit the time and space needed to set up safe zones and protected, safe-passage corridors so refugees can return and humanitarian aid can be provided.

---

[4] For a more detailed study of mapping the spread of violence, see John O'Laughlin et al., "The Afghanistan-Pakistan Wars, 2008–2009; Micrographics, Conflict Diffusion, and Clusters of Violence," *Eurasian Geography and Economics,* 2010, Vol. 51, No. 4, pp. 437–471.

These measures are likely to require the presence of some type of international stabilization force and a partial no-fly zone.[5] They also are likely to require acknowledging that Assad may have to be part of the solution and that Syria and Iraq may have to be partitioned. No border is sacrosanct.

Policy measures that are focused solely on the effects of the spill-over (such as helping Turkey, Lebanon, and Jordan deal with the flow of refugees within their borders) are unlikely to be sufficient—like a doctor treating only the visible symptoms of an infectious disease: The patient and others standing nearby will continue to be at risk.

To come full circle: All roads lead to Damascus and back out again, but in different ways and in different directions. With hundreds of jihadists from Europe, Russia, the Arab Gulf, and the United States fighting in Syria, Europe and the rest of the West and Arab Gulf States become likely return destinations for them and the skills they have acquired. [6]

---

[5]   Mueller, Karl P., Jeffrey Martini, and Thomas Hamilton, *Air Power Options for Syria: Assessing Objectives and Missions for Aerial Intervention,* Santa Monica, Calif.: RAND Corporation, RR-446-CMEPP, September 2013.

[6]   Ben Hubbard et al., "Power Vacuum in Middle East Lifts Militants," *New York Times,* January 5, 2014, p. 1.

References

"4 Killed in Twin Suicide Blasts in Beirut," *Washington Post,* February 2014, p. 10.

Adams, Henry, "BACKGROUND: Iraqi Kurdistan Backing Syrian Rebels While Baghdad Supports Assad Online," United for Peace of Pierce County website, December 28, 2012. As of May 21, 2014:
http://www.ufppc.org/us-a-world-news-mainmenu-35/11330-background-iraqi-kurdistan-backing-syrian-rebels-while-baghdad-supports-assad.html

Addison, Tony, and S. Mansoob Murshed, *Transnational Terrorism as a Spillover of Domestic Disputes in Other Countries,* World Institute for Development Economics, December 2002.

Adnan, Duraid, "Massacre of Syrian Soldiers in Iraq Raises Risk of Widening Conflict," *New York Times,* March 4, 2013.

Ajami, Fouad, *The Syrian Rebellion,* Stanford: Hoover Institution Press, 2012.

Al-Najar, Mohammad, "Al-Nusra in Syria Learned From Lessons Passed," *al-Jazeera* (Arabic source), May 2013. As of May 21, 2014:
http://www.aljazeera.net/news/pages/e4ec8d8a-ead8-4132-9299-7ce2d9e458e2

———, "Syrian Front 'Melts' in Anticipation of US Strike," *al-Jazeera* (Arabic source), September 2013. As of May 21, 2014:
http://www.aljazeera.net/news/pages/5438676d-7d97-4238-8816-ea97b023f4b9

Amos, Deborah, and David Greene, "How Food Aid Is Being Used As A Weapon In Syria," National Public Radio, July 29, 2013. As of May 28, 2014:
http://www.npr.org/templates/story/story.php?storyId=206555367

Arabic Sky News, "A Dispute over Integrating Al-Nusra Front to AQI," June 2013.

Arango, Tim, "Syrian War's Spillover Threatens a Fragile Iraq," *New York Times,* September 24, 2012.

———, "A Re-Ignited War Drives Iraqis Out in Huge Numbers," *New York Times,* June 29, 2014.

Aras, Nisan Su, "Turkey May Host 1 million Syrian Refugees by 2014," *Hurriyet Daily News,* June 21, 2013. As of May 20, 2014:
http://www.hurriyetdailynews.com/Default.aspx?pageID=238&nid=49206

Assir, Serene, "Tripoli Clashes: Keeping Conflict Alive," *al-Akhbar,* February 2012. As of May 20, 2014:
http://english.al-akhbar.com/node/4158

Atlas, Terry, "Foreign Fighters Flocking to Syria Stirs Terror Concerns," Bloomberg News, July 20, 2013. As of May 28, 2014:
http://www.bloomberg.com/news/2013-07-19/u-s-stakes-in-syria-grow-as-radicals-rally-to-the-fight.html

Atzili, Boaz, "When Good Fences Make Bad Neighbors: Fixed Borders, State Weakness, and International Conflict," *International Security,* Vol. 31, No. 3, Winter 2006/07, pp. 139–173.

Balci, Bayram, "Turkish Protests, Syria Crisis Will Boost Turkey-PKK Peace Process." *World Politics Review,* July 29, 2013. As of May 20, 2014:
http://carnegieendowment.org/2013/07/29/turkish-protests-syria-crisis-will-boost-turkey-pkk-peace-process/ggqq

Barnard, Anne, "Swollen With Syrian Refugees, Lebanon Feels Its Stitching Fray," *New York Times,* February 23, 2013. As of May 21, 2014:
http://www.nytimes.com/2013/02/24/world/middleeast/syrian-flood-into-lebanon-stirs-fear-of-looming-disaster.html

Baydar, Yavuz, "Bombing Exposes Divide in Turkish Politics," *al Monitor,* May 14, 2013. As of May 20, 2014:
http://www.al-monitor.com/pulse/originals/2013/05/turkey-bombing-divide-politics.html

Bayoumy, Yara, "Lebanon Needs $20 Billion for Infrastructure," Reuters, October 20, 2010. As of May 21, 2014:
http://www.reuters.com/article/2010/10/20/us-mideast-summit-lebanon-infrastructure-idUSTRE69J3MB20101020

Beardsley, Kyle, "Peacekeeping and the Contagion of Armed Conflict," *Journal of Politics,* Vol. 73, No. 4, October 2011, pp. 1051–1064.

Berman, Sheri, "The Promise of the Arab Spring In Political Development, No Gain Without Pain," *Foreign Affairs,* January/February 2013.

Betts, Richard, "The Delusion of Impartial Intervention," *Foreign Affairs,* November/December 1994.

"Blast Kills Dozens in Turkish Town Reyhanli on Syria Border," BBC News, May 11, 2013. As of May 20, 2014:
http://www.bbc.co.uk/news/world-middle-east-22494128

Bosker, Maarten, and Joppe de Reey, *Localizing Conflict Spillovers: Introducing Regional Heterogeneity in Conflict Studies,* University of Groningen, 2009. As of May 19, 2014:
http://www.csae.ox.ac.uk/conferences/2009-EDiA/papers/346-deRee.pdf

Booth, William, "Group Linked to al-Qaida Claims Rocket Attack on Israel," *Washington Post,* August 23, 2013, p. A11.

———, "Jordan Keeping a Wary Eye on Israeli-Palestinian Talks," *Washington Post,* February 14, 2014, p. 8.

Booth, William, and Taylor Luck, "In Jordan, Concern Over the Allure of ISIS," *Washington Post,* June 29, 2014.

Booth, William, and Loveday Morris, "Alleged Chemical Attack Leaves One Family Reeling," *Washington Post,* August 26, 2013.

Braha, Dan, "Global Civil Unrest: Contagion, Self-Organization, and Prediction," *PLoS ONE,* Vol. 7, No. 10, October 2012.

Braithwaite, Alex, "Resisting Infection: How State Capacity Conditions Conflict Contagion," *Journal of Peace Research,* Vol. 47, No. 3, 2010, pp. 311–319.

Brennan, Margret, "Al Qaeda in Iraq Has Shifted Base of Operations to Syria, State Dept. Says," CBS News, August 13, 2013.

Buhaug, Halvard, "Geography, Rebel Capability, and the Duration of Civil Conflict," *Journal of Conflict Resolution,* 2009, pp. 544–569.

Buhaug, Halvard, and Kristian Skrede Gleditsch, "Contagion or Confusion? Why Conflicts Cluster in Space," *International Studies Quarterly,* 2008, pp. 215–233.

Butler, Daren, "Kurdish Militants in War of Words with Turkey Over Withdrawal." Reuters, August 19, 2013. As of May 20, 2014:
http://www.reuters.com/article/2013/08/19/
us-turkey-kurds-idUSBRE97I0C620130819

Byman, Daniel, Peter Chalk, Bruce Hoffman, William Rosenau, and David Brannan, *Trends in Outside Support for Insurgent Movements,* Santa Monica, Calif.: RAND Corporation, MR-1405-OTI, 2001. As of May 15, 2014:
http://www.rand.org/pubs/monograph_reports/MR1405.html

Byman, Daniel, and Kenneth Pollack, *Things Fall Apart: Containing the Spillover from an Iraqi Civil War,* Washington, D.C.: Brookings Institution Press, 2007.

Cagaptay, Soner, "Syria's War Could Inflame Turkey's Hatay Province," Washington Institute for Near East Policy, Policywatch 2063, April 4, 2013. As of May 20, 2014:
http://www.washingtoninstitute.org/policy-analysis/view/
syrias-war-could-inflame-turkeys-hatay-province

"Charbel: Over 2 million Syrians in Lebanon by End Year!" *Middle East Times,* July 30, 2013. As of May 20, 2014: http://www.mideast-times.com/home_news.php?newsid=5381

Coalition Provisional Authority, Order 51, Suspension of Exclusive Agency Status of Iraqi State Company for Water Transportation, May 16, 2003.

Collier, P., and A. Hoeffler, *Greed and Grievance in Civil War,* World Bank Policy Research Working Paper 2355, World Bank, Washington, D.C., 2001

Collier, Paul, et al., "On the Duration of Civil War," *Journal of Peace Research,* Vol. 41, No. 3, May, 2004, pp. 253–273.

Cordesman, Anthony, *Iran's Revolutionary Guards, the Al-Quds Force, and Other Intelligence and Paramilitary Forces,* Center for Strategic and International Studies, August 16, 2007, p. 9. As of July 11, 2014: http://csis.org/files/media/csis/pubs/070816_cordesman_report.pdf

Danneman, Nathan, and Emily Hencken Ritter, "Contagious Rebellion and Preemptive Repression," *Journal of Conflict Resolution,* January 20, 2013, p. 3.

Dorell, Oren, "Turkey: 9 with Syrian Ties Arrested in Car Bombings," *USA Today,* May 12, 2013. As of May 20, 2014: http://www.usatoday.com/story/news/world/2013/05/12/turkey-syria-car-bombings/2153245/

Fahim, Kareem, and Sebnem Arsu, "Car Bombings Kill Dozens in Center of Turkish Town Near the Syrian Border," *New York Times,* May 11, 2013. As of May 20, 2014: http://www.nytimes.com/2013/05/12/world/middleeast/bombings-in-turkish-border-town.html?_r=0

Fearon, J. D., and D.D. Laitin, "Ethnicity, Insurgency, and Civil War," *American Political Science Review,* 2003, pp. 75–90.

Findley, Michael G., "Rethinking Third-Party Interventions into Civil Wars: An Actor-Centric Approach," *Journal of Politics,* Vol. 68, No. 4, November 2006, pp. 828–837.

Fischer, Hannah, *Iraqi Civilian Death Estimates,* Congressional Research Service, RS22537, August 27, 2008. As of May 21, 2014: http://www.fas.org/sgp/crs/mideast/RS22537.pdf

foreignpolicy.com, *Failed States,* undated. As of May 21, 2014: http://www.foreignpolicy.com/articles/2013/06/24/2013_failed_states_interactive_map

Forman, Eric M., "Civil War as a Source of International Violence," *Journal of Politics,* Vol. 34, No. 4, November 1972, pp. 1111–1134.

Forsberg, Erika, "Polarization and Ethnic Conflict in a Widened Strategic Setting," *Journal of Peace Research,* Vol. 45, No. 2, 2008, pp. 283–300.

Galey, Patrick, "Lebanon: Passing the Failed State Test," *al-Akhbar,* July 20, 2012. As of May 21, 2014:
http://english.al-akhbar.com/node/10088

Gard-Murray, Alexander S., and Yaneer Bar-Yam, "Complexity and the Limits of Revolution: What Will Happen to the Arab Spring?" *New England Complex Systems Institute,* December 11, 2012.

Gates, Sara, "Human Rights Risk Atlas 2013: Maplecroft Releases Annual Ranking Of Countries At Risk Of Human Rights Violations," Huffington Post, December 13, 2012. As of May 21, 2014:
http://www.huffingtonpost.com/2012/12/13/human-rights-index-2013-maplecroft-human-rights-violations_n_2287960.html#slide=1874660

Gettleman, Jeffrey, "As Syria War Roils, Unrest Among Sects Hits Turkey," *New York Times,* August 4, 2012. As of May 20, 2014:
http://www.nytimes.com/2012/08/05/world/middleeast/turkish-alawites-fear-spillover-of-violence-from-syria.html?pagewanted=all&_r=0

Gleditsch, Kristian Skrede, *All International Politics is Local,* Ann Arbor: The University of Michigan Press, 2002.

————, "Fighting at Home, Fighting Abroad: How Civil Wars Lead to International Disputes," *Journal of Conflict Resolution,* April 1, 2008.

Erdem Güneş, "Death Toll Rises to 50 as Explosions Hit Turkish Town on Border with Syria," *Hurriyet Daily News,* May 11, 2013. As of May 20, 2014:
http://www.hurriyetdailynews.com/explosions-hit-turkish-town-on-border-with-syria-killing-four-and-injuring-18.aspx?pageID=238&nID=46682&NewsCatID=341

"Factbox: Iraq's Military Strength," Reuters, December 11, 2011. As of May 21, 2014:
http://www.reuters.com/article/2011/12/11/
us-iraq-withdrawal-military-idUSTRE7BA0GS20111211

Gerson, Michael, "The Reluctant Refuge," *Washington Post,* August 23, 2013, p. A19.

————, "War's Exacting Toll," *Washington Post,* August 27, 2013, p. A17.

Haass, Richard N., "Ripeness of Conflict: A Fruitful Notion?" *Journal of Peace Research,* Vol. 31, No. 1, February 1994, pp. 109–116.

Herrmann, Richard, and Jong Kun Choi, "From Prediction to Learning: Opening Experts' Minds to Unfolding History," *International Security,* Spring 2007, p. 132.

Hopkins, Rebecca A., "Lebanon and the Uprising in Syria: Issue for Congress," Congressional Research Service, February 2, 2012, p. 9. As of May 28, 2014:
https://www.fas.org/sgp/crs/mideast/R42339.pdf

Houweling, Hank, and Jan Siccama, "The Epidemiology of War, 1816–1980," *Journal of Conflict Resolution,* Vol. 29, 1985, pp. 641–662.

Hubbard, Ben, and a New York Times employee, "Kurdish Struggle Blurs Syria's Battle Lines," *New York Times,* August 1, 2013. As of May 20, 2014: http://www.nytimes.com/2013/08/02/world/middleeast/syria.html?_r=0

Hubbard, Ben, and Hwaida Saad, "Deadly Blast Rocks a Hizbollah Stronghold in Lebanon," *New York Times,* August 16, 2013, p. A4.

Hubbard, Ben, et al., "Power Vacuum in Middle East Lifts Militants," *New York Times,* January 5, 2014, p. 1.

International Crisis Group, "Blurring the Borders: Syrian Spillover Risks for Turkey," Europe Report No. 225, April 30, 2013.

"Iraq: Strikes Spread Beyond Anbar," *New York Times,* February 12, 2014, p. 6.

"Israel: al-Qaeda Plot Against U.S. Embassy Alleged," *Washington Post,* January 23, 2014.

Itani, Faysal, "Beyond Spillover: Syria's Role in Lebanon's Drift Toward Political Violence," Atlantic Counsel Issue Brief, July 2013. As of May 19, 2014: http://www.acus.org/files/publication_pdfs/403/beyond_spillover.pdf

Jones, Seth, "The Mirage of the Arab Spring," *Foreign Affairs,* Vol. 92, No. 1, January 2013, pp. 55–63.

Kart, Emine, "Turkey Not Categorically Against Formation of Autonomous Kurdish Entity Inside Syria," *Hurriyet Daily News,* August 16, 2013. As of May 20, 2014: http://www.hurriyetdailynews.com/turkey-not-categorically-against-formation-of-autonomous-kurdish-entity-inside-syria.aspx?pageID=238&nID=52627&NewsCatID=352

Kazimi, Nibras, *Syria Through Jihadist Eyes: A Perfect Enemy,* Stanford: Hoover Institution Press, 2010.

Keclera, Kelly, "Transmission, Barriers, and Constraints: A Dynamic Model of the Spread of War," *Journal of Conflict Resolution,* Vol. 42, 1998, pp. 367–387.

Khondker, Habibul Haque, "Role of the New Media in the Arab Spring," Zayed University, Abu Dhabi, United Arab Emirates. November 18, 2011.

Kleiboer. Marieke, "Ripeness of Conflict: A Fruitful Notion?" (review), *Journal of Peace Research,* Vol. 31, No. 1, February 1994, pp. 109–116.

Kratochwil, Friedrich, "Of Systems, Boundaries, and Territoriality: An Inquiry into the Formation of the State System," *Politics,* Vol. 39, No. 1, October 1986, pp. 27–52.

Lacina, Bethany, "Explaining the Severity of Civil Wars," *Journal of Conflict Resolution,* Vol. 50, 2006, p. 276.

Lake, David, and Donald S. Rothchild, *The International Spread of Ethnic Conflict: Fear, Diffusion, and Escalation,* Princeton: Princeton University Press, 1998.

Larrabee, Stephen F., "Is Turkey Rethinking the Syrian Kurd issue?" *CNN Global Public Square,* August 21, 2013. As of May 20, 2014:
http://globalpublicsquare.blogs.cnn.com/2013/08/21/
is-turkey-rethinking-the-syrian-kurd-issue/

"Lebanon Sentences al-Nusra Members to Death," *al-Alam,* July 19, 2013. As of May 21, 2014:
http://en.alalam.ir/news/1496447

Letsch, Constanze, "Syrian Refugee Crisis Raises Tensions in Turkish Border Towns," *The Guardian,* July 25, 2013. As of May 20, 2014:
http://www.theguardian.com/world/2013/jul/25/
syrian-refugee-crisis-tensions-turkey

Licklider, R, and R.H. Wagner, "The Consequences of Negotiated Settlements in Civil Wars, 1945–1993," *American Political Science Review,* Vol. 89, No.3. September 1995.

Luca, Ana Maria, "A Different Type of Spillover," *NOW,* April 19, 2013. As of May 20, 2014:
https://now.mmedia.me/lb/en/reportsfeatures/a-different-type-of-spillover

Luttwak, Edward N., "Give War a Chance," *Foreign Affairs,* Vol. 78, No. 4 July/August 1999, pp. 36–44.

Mahmoud, Muna, and Martin Chulov, "Syrian War Widens Sunni-Shia Schism as Foreign Jihadis Join Fight for Shrines," *The Guardian,* June 4, 2013.

Martini, Jeffrey, Erin York, William Young, *Syria as an Arena of Strategic Competition,* Santa Monica, Calif.: RAND Corporation, RR-213-OSD, 2013. As of May 15, 2014: http://www.rand.org/pubs/research_reports/RR213.html

Maves, Jessica, "Autocratic Institutions and Civil Conflict Contagion," *Journal of Politics,* Vol. 75, No. 2, April 2013, pp. 478–490.

McDonnell, Patrick, "Free Syrian Army Will Shift Headquarters from Turkey to Syria," *Los Angeles Times,* September 23, 2012.

"Media in Lebanon: Reporting on a Nation Divided," IPI, December 2006.

Melki, Jad, et al., "Mapping Digital Media: Lebanon," Open Society Foundation, March 15, 2012. As of May 21, 2014:
http://www.opensocietyfoundations.org/sites/default/files/mapping-digital-media-lebanon-20120506.pdf

Midlarsky, Manus I., "Analyzing Diffusion and Contagion Effects: The Urban Disorders of the 1960s," *American Political Science Review,* Vol. 72, No. 3, September 1978, pp. 996–1008.

Midlarsky, Manus, et al., "Why Violence Spreads: The Contagion of International Terrorism," *International Studies Quarterly,* Vol. 24, No. 2. June 1980, pp. 262–298.

Morris, Loveday, and Suzan Haidamous, "Bomb Kills at Least 18 in Beirut," *Washington Post,* August 16, 2013, p. A8.

Morris, Loveday, and Ahmed Ramadan, "Blasts Kill at Least 27 in Lebanon," *Washington Post,* August 24, 2013, p. A1.

Mueller, Karl P., Jeffrey Martini, and Thomas Hamilton, *Air Power Options for Syria: Assessing Objectives and Missions for Aerial Intervention,* Santa Monica, Calif.: RAND Corporation , RR-446-CMEPP, September 2013. As of June 17, 2014: http://www.rand.org/pubs/research_reports/RR446.html

Murdoch, James C., and Todd Sandler, "Economic Growth, Civil Wars, and Spatial Spillovers," *Journal of Conflict Resolution,* 2002, pp. 91–110.

Naufal, Hala, "Syrian Refugees in Lebanon: the Humanitarian Approach Under Political Divisions," Migration Policy Centre, 2012/2013 Report, 2012. As of May 20, 2014:
http://cadmus.eui.eu/handle/1814/24835

Nerguzian, Aram, "The Lebanese Armed Forces: Challenges and Opportunities in Post-Syria Lebanon." CSIS, February 10, 2009. As of May 21, 2014:
http://csis.org/files/media/csis/pubs/090210_lafsecurity.pdf

NOW, *Lebanon-Syria Borders: 2009 Report, web page,* undated. As of May 20, 2014:
https://now.mmedia.me/Library/Files/EnglishDocumentation/Other%20 Documents/Border%20Report%20NOW.pdf

O'Laughlin, John, et al., "The Afghanistan-Pakistan Wars, 2008–2009; Micrographics, Conflict Diffusion, and Clusters of Violence," *Eurasian Geography and Economics,* 2010, Vol. 51, No. 4, pp. 437–471.

Pamuk, Humeyra, "Turkey Plays Big in Kurdistan's Energy Game," Reuters, August 15, 2013. As of May 20, 2014:
http://www.reuters.com/article/2013/08/15/ us-iraq-kurdistan-idUSBRE97E0RC20130815

Pearce, Fred, "Youthquake," *New Scientist,* July 20, 2013, pp. 42–45.

"PYD Begins Fight Against al-Assad Regime Forces in Northern Syria," *Hurriyet Daily News,* April 8, 2013. As of May 20, 2014:
http://www.hurriyetdailynews.com/pyd-begins-fight-against-al-assad-regime-forces-in-northern-syria.aspx?pageID=238&nid=44480

Quammen, David, *Spillover: Animal Infections and the Next Pandemic,* New York: W.W. Norton & Company, 2012, p. 43.

Regan, Patrick M., "Third-Party Interventions and the Duration of Intrastate Conflicts," *Journal of Conflict Resolution,* Vol. 46, 2002.

Remnick, David, "Letter from Jordan: City of the Lost," *New Yorker,* August 26, 2013, pp. 49–57.

"Reyhanli Bombings Death Toll Reaches 52," *Hurriyet Daily News,* May 27, 2013. As of May 20, 2014:
http://www.hurriyetdailynews.com/reyhanli-bombings-death-toll-reaches-52.aspx?pageID=238&nID=47671&NewsCatID=341

"Rising Tide of Refugees," *Christian Science Monitor Weekly,* June 2, 2014, p. 12.

Rosen, Armin, "Turkey's Camps Can't Expand Fast Enough for All the New Syrian Refugees," *The Atlantic,* April 18, 2013. As of May 20, 2014:
http://www.theatlantic.com/international/archive/2013/04/turkeys-camps-cant-expand-fast-enough-for-all-the-new-syrian-refugees/275125/

Saab, Bilal Y., "The Syrian Spillover and Salafist Radicalization in Lebanon," CTC Sentinel, July 23, 2013. As of May 21, 2014:
http://www.ctc.usma.edu/posts/the-syrian-spillover-and-salafist-radicalization-in-lebanon

Saad, Hwaida, and Ben Hubbard, "Lebanon Forms a Cabinet After 11 Months of Deadlock," *New York Times,* February 16, 2014, p. 8.

Saideman, Stephen M., "When Conflict Spreads: Arab Spring and the Limits of Contagion," *International Interactions,* Vol. 37, No. 5, 2012.

Salehyan, Idean, and Kristian Skrede Gleditsch, "Refugees and the Spread of Civil War," *International Organization,* Vol. 60, No. 2, April 2006, pp. 335–366.

Salvatore, Armando, "Before (and After) the 'Arab Spring': From Connectedness to Mobilization in the Public Sphere" *Oriente Moderno,* Vol. 91, No. 1, 2011, pp. 5–12.

Samaha, Nour, "Is Lebanon Spiralling Out of Control?" *al-Jazeera,* June 21, 2013. As of May 21, 2014:
http://www.aljazeera.com/indepth/features/2013/06/201362013123581912.html

Sambanis, Nicholas, "What Is Civil War? Conceptual and Empirical Complexities of an Operational Definition," *Journal of Conflict Resolution,* Vol. 48, 2004.

Shrek, Adam, "Iraqi Shiite Fighters' Role in Syria Grows More Prominent, Raising Sectarian Tensions at Home," Associated Press, June 10, 2013. As of May 21, 2014:
http://www.foxnews.com/world/2013/06/10/iraqi-shiite-fighters-role-in-syria-grows-more-prominent-raising-sectarian/#ixzz2dJvSIgOK

Sly, Liz, and Loveday Morris, "Militants Announce Creation of a Formal Islamic State," *Washington Post,* June 30, 2014.

Stack, Liam, "In Slap at Syria, Turkey Shelters Anti-Assad Fighters," *New York Times,* October 27, 2011. As of May 28, 2014:
http://www.nytimes.com/2011/10/28/world/europe/turkey-is-sheltering-antigovernment-syrian-militia.html?pagewanted=all&_r=0

Starr, Harvey, " 'Opportunity' and 'Willingness' as Ordering Concepts in the Study of War," *International Interactions,* Vol. 4, 1978, pp. 363–387.

———, "Opportunity and Willingness and the Nexus Between Internal and External Conflict," paper prepared for presentation at the Annual Meeting of the Western Political Science Association, Seattle, March 20–23, 1991.

Stedman, Stephen J., *Peacemaking in Civil War: International Mediation in Zimbabwe, 1974–1980,* Lynne Rienner Publishers, 1991.

syrftr.com, "Syria the Future, A Jordanian Salafi Leader Estimates Al-Nusra Fighters at 12,000," April 2013.

"Syria's Islamist Fighters: Competition Among Islamists," *The Economist,* July 20, 2013.

Target Group Index Lebanon, "Lebanon Internet Scene," 2009, market research report by Media Direction OMD, via OSF 2012 Report.

Taylor, Julie, "Leave Hezbollah Alone!" *Foreign Policy,* July 24, 2013. As of May 21, 2014:
http://mideast.foreignpolicy.com/posts/2013/07/24/leave_hezbollah_alone

Tejel, Jordi, "Syria's Kurds: Troubled Past, Uncertain Future," Carnegie Endowment for International Peace, October 16, 2012. As of May 20, 2014:
http://carnegieendowment.org/2012/10/16/syria-s-kurds-troubled-past-uncertain-future/e2nt

Terrill, W. Andrew, "Regional Spillover Effects of the Iraq War," Strategic Studies Institute, December 2008.

"Time Explains: How Syria's War is Reviving Al Qaeda in Iraq," *Time,* undated. As of May 21, 2014:
http://content.time.com/time/video/player/0,32068,2586624786001_2148880,00.html#ixzz2dRXkJ3Zo

Toft, Monica Duffy, "Ending Civil Wars: A Case for Rebel Victory?" *International Security,* Vol. 34, No. 4, Spring 2010, pp. 7–36.

Torchia, Christopher, and Mehmet Guzel, "Turkey Seeks to Relocate Some Syrian Refugees," Associated Press, September 16, 2012. As of May 20, 2014:
http://news.yahoo.com/turkey-seeks-relocate-syrian-refugees-101427401.html

Too Close For Comfort: Syrians in Lebanon, Crisis Group, Middle East Report. May 2013. As of May 20, 2014:
http://www.crisisgroup.org/~/media/Files/Middle%20East%20North%20Africa/Iraq%20Syria%20Lebanon/Lebanon/141-too-close-for-comfort-syrians-in-lebanon.pdf

Totten, Michael, "The Beginning of the End for Hezbollah," *World Affairs,* April 22, 2013. As of May 21, 2014:
http://www.worldaffairsjournal.org/blog/michael-j-totten/beginning-end-hezbollah

Transparency International, *Corruption Perceptions Index,* country results, undated. As of May 21, 2014:
http://cpi.transparency.org/cpi2012/results/

"UN Aid for Refugees in Syria, Iraqi Kurdistan," *al-Jazeera* (Arabic), August 27, 2013. As of May 21, 2014:
http://www.aljazeera.net/news/pages/15be6f16-9bf2-4218-8088-11fe8daa1ab6

United Nations Development Report, *Human Development Report 2013, The Rise of the South: Human Progress in a Diverse World,* undated. As of May 21, 2014:
http://www.undp.org/content/dam/undp/library/corporate/HDR/2013GlobalHDR/English/HDR2013%20Report%20English.pdf

UNHCR—*See* United Nations High Commissioner for Refugees.

United Nations High Commissioner for Refugees, *Syria Regional Refugee Response,* web page, undated. As of May 20, 2014: http://data.unhcr.org/syrianrefugees/country.php?id=122

———, "UNHCR Turkey Syrian Refugee Daily Sitrep," August 20, 2013. As of May 20, 2014:
http://data.unhcr.org/syrianrefugees/download.php?id=2622

United Nations Security Council, Resolutions 1559 and 1680.

Walter, Barbara F., "Building Reputation: Why Governments Fight Some Separatists But Not Others," *American Journal of Political Science,* Vol. 50, No. 2, 2006, pp. 313–330.

Warrick, Joby, "Influx of Syrian Refugees Stretches Jordan's Water Resources Even More Thinly," *Washington Post,* June 16, 2013. As of May 19, 2014:
http://www.washingtonpost.com/world/national-security/influx-of-syrian-refugees-stretches-jordans-water-resources-even-thinner/2013/06/15/5178a978-d2c6-11e2-a73e-826d299ff459_print.html

"With Syria In Shambles, the Uncertain Future of Hezbollah." NPR, February 26, 2013.

World Bank, *World Development Indicators,* 2012.

World Security Network, "Syrian Kurds Given Military Training In Northern Iraq, Says Barzani," October 25, 2012. As of May 21, 2014:
http://www.worldsecuritynetwork.com/Syria/Todays-Zaman/
Syrian-Kurds-given-military-training-in-northern-Iraq-says-Barzani

Worth, Robert, "Lawless Sinai Shows Risks Rising in Fractured Egypt," *New York Times,* August 11, 2013, p. A1.

Young, William, *The Winners and Losers From The Syria Conflict,* cnn.com, January 21, 2013. As of May 15, 2014:
http://globalpublicsquare.blogs.cnn.com/2013/01/31/
the-winners-and-losers-from-the-syria-conflict/

Zartman, I. William, *Ripe for Resolution: Conflict and Intervention in Africa,* Oxford University Press, 1989.

Zirulnick, Ariel, "The Five Most Dangerous Countries for Journalists," *Christian Science Monitor,* undated. As of May 21, 2014:
http://www.csmonitor.com/World/Global-Issues/2010/1108/
The-five-most-dangerous-countries-for-journalists/Iraq